Healing, Purifying, and Manifesting through the Ancient Chinese Art of Qigong (Chi Gong)

Various Articles on Physical, Emotional, and Spiritual Healing

By Salvatore Canzonieri
– Jindao Life Transforming Qigong

publisher

BGT ENT

writer/editor

Sal Canzonieri

publication design

BGT ENT - SAL CANZONIERI

Healing, Purifying, and Manifesting through the Ancient Chinese Art of Qigong (Chi Gong) -
Various Articles on Physical, Emotional, and Spiritual Healing

sponsored by

Jin Dao Life

www.JinDaoLife.com / www.bgtent.com

First edition: January 2013

10 9 8 7 6 5 4 3 2 1

Digital Version

ACKNOWLEDGEMENTS

Thanks to Sue Freeman- Art of the Heart, Chester NJ; Madelyn – Growing with the Seasons, Boonton, NJ; Lillian – Sages Pages, Madison NJ, and all the many people involved with Jin Dao Life Qigong, Neigong, and Daoyin classes and healing sessions.

Healing, Purifying, and Manifesting through the Ancient Chinese Art of Qigong (Chi Gong) - Various Articles on Physical, Emotional, and Spiritual Healing

Articles

The Jin Dao Life System

What is Qigong Therapy?

by Salvatore Canzonieri

Qigong (pronounced as Chee Gung) is also known as Chinese Yoga, or as Neigong (Internal Exercises), which is more like a Chinese version of Pilates.

A definition of Qigong is: an internal meditation method using moving and standing exercises practiced to promote the movement of vital energy throughout the body.

Qigong increases internal cleansing and purifying and has been known to help remove many ailments and improve one's health tremendously.

Qigong is a practice that often uses slow graceful movements and controlled breathing techniques to promote the circulation of energy within the human body, and enhance a practitioner's overall health. Qigong's gentle movements, meditation, and breathing techniques cleanse and strengthen the immune system and Life Energy (Qi).

The ideas and movements originated thousands of years ago in China. There are also many forms of Qigong that are done with little or no movement at all, in standing, sitting, and lying positions; likewise, not all forms of Qigong use breath control techniques.

There are more than 10,000 styles of qigong and 200 million people practicing these methods.

Why practice Qigong & Neigong?

There are three main reasons why people practice Qigong:
1) To gain strength, improve health, or reverse a disease;
2) To gain skill working with qi, so as to become a healer;
3) To become more connected with the "Tao, God, True Source, Great Spirit", for a more meaningful spiritual connection with nature and the universe.

Benefits of Qigong & Neigong:

- Boost your health & vitality - improves nervous system function;
- Gain peace of mind - clears negative emotions and reduces anxiety;
- Promote longevity & total wellness;
- Relieve stress - drops stress hormone (salivary cortisol) levels;
- Promote deeper relaxation and better sleep;
- Achieve greater aerobic capacity;
- Weight loss and stay fit - regulates digestion and metabolism;
- Heal internal injuries;
- Prevent osteoporosis;
- A stronger and more limber body - increases flexibility and mobility;
- Become more confident and clear minded
- Aerobic exercise recommended for coronary artery disease;
- Lower your blood pressure;
- Increase your strength and stamina;
- Gain confidence and self control;
- Become better able to focus;
- Improve your daily performance;
- Release negative emotions & gain positive feelings;
- Become more sensitive to energy changes in the environment;
- Improve your sports skills (golf, tennis, baseball, basketball, football, wrestling, MMA, etc.);
- Protecting yourself and your loved ones.

"We practice Qigong to complement our lives – not to restrict or limit our lives. If you could do something before you practiced Qigong and enjoy it, then you will be able to do it even better after practicing Qigong." - Marcus Santer

---

Benefits of Qigong - June 20, 2010

What benefits you can expect to gain if you practice Qigong (Chi Gong):

1. **Health and Vitality** – improve health by removing blockages to harmonious chi/energy flow through the meridians of the body and then increase the flow of Qi resulting in vitality.

2. **Longevity** – Qigong starts by promoting smooth Qi flow = health, then vigorous Qi flow = vitality and then an abundance of Qi = Longevity.

3. **Internal Force** – Energy+ it helps you keep going all day long without feeling tired or fatigued.

4. **Mind Expansion** – clarity of thinking, enhanced problem solving etc

5. **Spiritual Cultivation** – for those who wish to, the practice of Qigong can help you to see and experience spiritual truths great spiritual masters have spoken about.

from Marcus Santer (check out his website: http://qigong365.com/)

Learning Qigong - Here's a note about progressing in the internal arts from a master - June 27, 2010

Only when you observe and feel with heart, carefully comparing, you can make it elegant and spirited. If you do not compare with others, you will never know. You will be surprised by the comparison. The enjoyment of learning comes from feeling the progress that you have made, from the differences between today and yesterday, from the changes that you never had before, from the principles that you never knew before. Mastering one is much better than knowing thousands. By comparing with yesterday, the day before yesterday, last week, and the first day, you will have more confidence and enjoyment.

The forte of Qigong is two fold - July 11, 2010

1) It **removes blockages** to the harmonious flow of energy through the meridians (channels) of your body thus restoring Yin Yang Harmony.

Whether these blockages are physical, emotional, mental, or spiritual in origin makes little difference to the effectiveness of Qigong.

2) Once energy blockages are removed, Qigong can then **increase the flow of energy** through the meridians promoting vitality and longevity.

This concise and clear quote about the purpose of Qigong is from Marcus Santer - check out his website: http://qigong365.com/

Qigong Breathing - July 18, 2010

Source: Francisco Gomes - http://holybreathspiritualqigong.com/

When you took your first breath of air as an infant you began to mix the original essence from our Kidneys with the energy from the air and food you absorbed from your mother to create life force energy and you were born. You used your lower abdominal muscles to deep breathe (belly breathe) with and stored the life force energy in our Lower Tan-Tien (dan-dee-en). Your Tan Tien is located 1.3 inches below the navel and 1/3 inside of your body and it's also called the Well of Water in Christianity, Hara in Japanese, Na'au in Hawaiian, Tewa in Tibetan, and Hypogastrium in Western Medicine.

You were a Spiritual being and from that moment on we began to constantly generate and store an abundance of life force in our Lower Tan Tien by lower abdominal deep breathing (Tan Tien Breathing) 24 hours day. The act of 24 hour abdominal (a Spiritual Holy Breath) breathing also increased the OHM vibration in your DNA which turned Matter into Spirit to purify you and this gave you a strong Spiritual connection with the One True Source (the Dao or Tao).

As you got older, more and more life force energy (living water) was stored in your Lower Tan-Tien. We had an abundance of life force energy stored in your Lower Tan Tien (living water well) in your youth. But, when you got older (4-14 years old) you reached a certain point when your 24 hour abdominal breathing (Tan Tien Breathing) (belly breathing) capabilities switched over to 16 hour or so a day shallow chest breathing due to eating and talking.

Let's take a breathing test: While standing up put one hand on your chest and the other on your lower abdomen just below your navel and inhale in through your nose. The hand on your chest moves. Lay down and put one hand on your chest and the other on your lower abdomen just below your navel, relax for a moment and inhale in through your nose. The hand on your lower abdomen will move (this is Lower Abdominal Deep Breathing, Tan Tien Breathing). Stand up and you will begin to shallow chest breathe again when you inhale.

When this happened you began to lose 2/3's of your Life Force supply to our Lower Tan Tien and the Spirit of the One True Source within began to weaken due to lack of life force inside your body. Qigong work re-awakens us to breathe as we originally did when we were infants, and thus this deep abdominal breathing (from the sides, to the back, to the front, to the top) opens our bodies and fills us with healing and purifying oxygen and removes stagnation and blockages, allowing us to live not only longer but healthier lives. This opening method begins the process of healing from the physical (integrating the mind and body), to the emotional (peace of mind), and finally to the spiritual (self transformation).

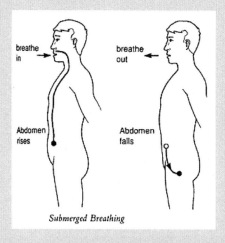

Submerged Breathing

About Qigong - August 1 , 2010

Source: Hilda Wei Williams http://www.chikung-unlimited.com/Benefits.html

- **Qigong develops tremendous mind power.** Few people outside of qigong circles have ever heard of the powers of *yinian* or the *yi* consciousness.

  It is the rudder or the steering wheel that channels the *chi* energy for healing, self-defense, will power and concentration, health and longevity, spiritual development, and so much more! When the *yi* consciousness is harnessed properly, the qigong practitioner is capable of unbelievably great power that far surpasses physical brute strength. A practitioner channels *chi* even further by extending it beyond the body, so that one is able to change how things are happening around you! This allows you to release blockages from past events to heal yourself, and also to change the energy so that you can manifest all that you desire (for the good of all). You became natural at doing things for the highest good, the more you give to more you get.

- How is this possible? Because qigong accesses the *yi* consciousness . Therein lies the mind power to harness and manipulate the *chi* life-force for self-defense, healing and personal development. Therein also lies the potential for developing unbelievable mind power.

- **Qigong develops psychic ability.** Some of the abilities manifested by qigong masters include psychic healing using *qi* or *chi* energy, distance healing, clairvoyance, telepathy, telekinesis, out-of-body experience (OBE), and soul travel.

A word about the PRACTICE of Qigong - August 8, 2010

Source: Hilda Wei Williams http://www.chikung-unlimited.com/Benefits.html

Without *Qi* energy there is no qigong. It is integral to why we practice qigong in the first place. And it is difficult for most people to conceptualize. To put it simply, it is a vital force or healing energy that is responsible for not just life, vitality, and health, but also personal development.

And it is the same life force that we employ when we transcend the physical plane to the higher levels of consciousness. At the highest level, we use only the *yinian*, mind power, also known as the *yi* consciousness to channel the life force.

Traditional qigong practices rely heavily on the cultivation of the *Qi* energy because of the many benefits that this healing energy produces.

It is the healing *Qi* that TCM doctors stimulate with acupuncture needles, acupressure massage and moxibustion. It is also healing energy tapped from the environment that the healer channels and transfers onto the person being healed.

Beginning students often tell me they feel tingling in their fingertips and attribute it to the beginning manifestations of this vital force. That is only a superficial experience. There are many different sensations, just as there are many different types of *Qi* energy and many of these sensations are far greater or subtler, and much more difficult to describe in words.

Instead of just physical well-being or specifically focused aspects of health, qigong views health at a much deeper, holistically, focusing the *Qi* energy for whole mind, body, and spiritual health, longevity, and healing.

And instead of merely increasing relaxation and concentration, traditional practices also seek to transcend the here and now, to attain a higher consciousness and to develop psychic power and abilities beyond what most can only imagine.

What is Qigong - August 14, 2010

"Qigong is the art of deliberately managing your vital energy. Vital energy is the force that enables you and everyone else to be alive. It is easier to learn than Tai Chi and less strenuous than Yoga. It usually combines simple external body movements with gentle breathing methods and is performed in a meditative state of mind. It is the oldest of the 5 branches of Traditional Chinese Medicine (TCM), practiced by millions of people daily worldwide and has a written record going back 5000 years. It requires zero athleticism or investment in equipment. If you can spare 10-15 minutes a day, you can practice this art.

In TCM, there is only one illness and that is Yin Yang disharmony. Or put another way, it means our body has failed in its natural ability to respond appropriately to disease causing agents. Fortunately **Good Health Is Your Birthright** and Yin Yang disharmony is unnatural. The great news is that: **From the TCM view of medicine there is no such thing as an incurable disease!** If we can restore the balance between Yin and Yang we will restore health."

from Marcus Santer (check out his website: http://qigong365.com/)

About the Nature of Qigong - August 21, 2010

Source: Luc Theler Hunyuan Qigong http://www.gongfu.ch/

Qigong goes back many thousands of years ago to an era when those who were wise were very closely connected with Nature and themselves. At that time, one was considered healthy when one lived in unity with the cosmos, and ill when one subdued one's own emotions. Animals were not enemies, but rather friends. Nature was not exploited, but rather respected. People schooled themselves in modesty and contemplation and learned from one another. Such people were the early fathers and mothers of these transformation techniques, which are aimed at living as one with the vast, unfathomable energy of Nature.

The natural scientist recognizes Nature's movement according to the law of polarity between the cosmic elemental forces of yin and yang. Thus, the spontaneous naturalness of life – everywhere and in every form – is the fundamental principle. Observe Nature when you are relaxed. Have you ever seen a straight rainbow? Have you ever watched a tadpole swim in a straight line? Or perhaps you have seen a straight cloud, a straight tree, a straight snake, a straight ravine, straight water, a straight head or spine or tongue? Everything which truly exists naturally is created in the shape of a wave. Every form of natural movement is like a wave, for everything undulates when viewed physically.

The dual but whole nature of Qi can be best imagined by placing oneself in front of a tree for an hour, remaining motionless and letting whatever happens happen. For one should not attempt to comprehend Qi intellectually, but rather to experience it. Look at the sky and you will see your inner space. Look into your inner space – and you will discover the sky. Three types of Qi are distinguished in the human being. The first is the prenatal Qi, which is produced from our genetic code (Jing) and gives our body its individual characteristics. In the second, we have the "acquired" Qi, the life energy, which we develop by eating and breathing. The third is the etheric Qi, which we produce through our thought and concentration potential. Qi is a term for the etheric life energy which contains life-giving light in various frequencies. The authentic teachings make it possible to synchronize these three circles of human vitality and thereby to harmonize them, thus enabling sheer vitality to unfold.

Furthermore, an incredible amount can be learned from the Qigong of animals. The primary factor in the Daoist teachings of transformation is as follows: storing, directing, regulating and refining life energy. Cats are masters of Qigong, for these predators are agile and flexible due to the storage, increase and sinking of Qi. Observe how a cat concentrates (Yi), collects its energy (Qi), and then leaps or attacks (fali). When you also consider the fact that cats always land on their feet due to their command of Qigong, you are left in awe.

In Buddhism one strives for a state of enlightenment, which is very abstract in the beginning and through deep meditation appears ever clearer. It is a future state of enlightenment (Nirvana) which the Buddhist searches for through the "purification" of his karma. In contrast, a Daoist himself strives to be spontaneous nature in the present moment and is therefore, with his endeavors, committed to the present. Daoists – like the Druids, the ancient magicians of Nature – have always viewed the light of creation as something spontaneous and inspiring. The creative human being is capable of producing the most Qi. For this reason, the practice of an art such as music, poetry, or painting was a fundamental component of the education of future priests of Nature both in the Daoistic as well as in the Druid teachings. Perfect tone, poetry, color, light and vibrations, find your elemental personal expression of creation and perfect your Being through perfecting the arts.

Qigong and the Yin Yang Symbol - August 28, 2010

Concerning Qigong, people look at the famous yin-yang symbol, but hardly realize what it means. It does not mean Balance, which is static and dead. It means **HARMONIC CHANGE**, like waves ebbing and flowing, always this way and that, bobbing and weaving about. Within each "fish" of the yin-yang symbol there is an "eye" or small circle, this means that whenever a force reaches an extreme, it contains within itself the seed of its own opposite. Hence, change is always there. Balance means there is no change. There is static, which means not harmony, but blockages, non-movements. Harmony is achieved like the striking of a tuning fork! The two sides of the fork are struck, and they sing out and vibrate. Their tones move in and out together creating a wavering tone, which hums like a happy song.

The humming comes from the change that came when the forks were struck. Change is flow, change is movement, and change is goodness. Every great come uppance was always first preceded by a great downfall - think back and you will see that in your life. The dips in your life were necessary for you to achieve the high points in your life, not only to appreciate them, but to actually generate them! IF there is stillness, static, then you don't notice anything, if there is change, then you become more aware, and more alive. The practice of Qigong allows you to generate change first in your hands, then inside, and then outside of yourself. Then, all good things flow to you and through you. When you realize that EVERYTHING is energy and vibrates together in a field of harmonious changes, then you draw what you desire to receive from the Dao, the One True Source, the Path, which is a field of unlimited possibilities. Qigong offers you life and to have it more abundantly.

Qigong is the Art of Energy - September 11, 2010

As we all know, EVERYTHING is made out of Energy / Qi. Not only objects but the space around objects is made of energy and thus filled with Qi. We're like fish swimming in water, they are unaware that they are immersed inside water; to them we are the ones swimming in air.

Because you are working to remove internal blockages to your harmonious flow of energy, when you practice your qigong movements, you not only are healing, purifying, and manifesting positive energy for yourself, but, since you are connected to all the energy around you, you are also doing these things to the space around you as well.

The more positive intention you put out and the more internal blockages you release from within, the more you are also healing the world around you and ultimately universal space, from the molecular to the stellar levels. As you radiate positive intentions, you are an antenna between Heaven and Earth. Heavenly energy always Gives (unconditional love) and Earthy energy always Receives. That is their nature, and they work in harmony with each other. People both give and receive, it is your true nature to be a sharing entity; the intersection of Heaven and Earth. Thus, to you and through you all good things come. As a result of your positive intentions (your desires) health, wealth, prosperity, and happiness are the RESULT of what your attention is focused on. The saying "Where attention goes, energy (Qi) flows", an often repeated quote, is an important thought to consider.

By increasing your sphere of effect, via sending out your positive intentions and focusing your attention on the results that come to you and through you, you affect all the energy around you. You supercharge your energy field and all the energy fields that come in contact with you. Through the practice of Qigong, you become a change agent, a means of transformation from negative to positive, a means for providing harmony to everything around you. Positive intentions bring Joy and Gratitude to all that is around you. Your sphere of influence brings harmony to all that touches it.

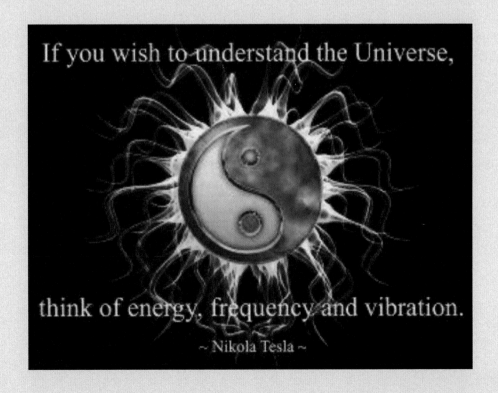

On the Nature of Giving and Receiving - September 18, 2010

In the Jindao Qigong system, the main idea is to connect with the Dao, the One True Source and align who we really are with how nature really is.

We heal and purify our energy fields so that we can manifest Joy in our lives. When we are in harmony with the Giving nature of the Heavens and with the Receiving nature of Earth> We feel at our best, we feel energetic, we feel strong. Our physical, emotional, and spiritual centers are united in a harmonious manner. In this state, you vibrate at a higher frequency causing you to glow; your body, heart/mind, and soul actually sing.

The RESULT of this harmonic Joy IS health, wealth, happiness, and prosperity. When you feel this Joy you are inspired to act, your inspired action brings results because you are always in the right place at the right time and you attract right people, right places, right possessions, and right prosperity. You feel Right. Feeling Joy allows one to focus attention towards the solution, not the problems behind us. This is called the Dao, the Way. It is the way, the path, that we walk on when we are not lost. Walking on this path we feel purpose and fulfillment. In this state, we already have ALL that is best for us, which we express as what we 'desire to receive'. We only have to accept it.

Giving energy is unconditional, always and ever, which we know as Love. This eternal Love is the very nature of the One True Source, from which all things have been created. Receiving energy is the very nature of the Earth, all things that exist on Earth return to it. The earth reclaims all things that exist on it. All things that exist on earth were created out of it from rock to plants to animals to people.

We can observe that Love creates. The act of Love creates many things: babies, art, music, sculptures, inventions, and more. But, Love must be received in order to be acknowledged and thus enjoyed. All of creation is not only the Vessel to receive this unconditional giving (Love), BUT, since all things come from the Source, all is composed of it. We are the full expression of the One True Source. Thus, Receiving comes from Giving.

Our physical center gives to the Earth; our spiritual center receives from the Heavens; our emotional center Shares with others, giving while receiving. When in the Qigong posture of Embracing The Moon, which looks like holding a cup in front in you, it appears as if you are both offering to others what is in your cup while at the same time your cup is being filled. The act is the same. Giving is Receiving. But, giving comes first. Just as the Universal Love creates, so too does Giving. Giving is a creative act. There is ONLY room to receive in your cup when you make room by giving. Hence, "The More you Give, the More you Receive". it is a Joyous thing to give, because it allows you to receive so much as well. By giving and receiving, we are able to manifest (create) all that is good for ourselves, for others, and for the world.

When we vibrate at the higher frequency of Joy, we naturally wish to express Gratitude to the Giving and Receiving Energies that intersect within us. When feeling Gratitude we can truly know that we are the Intersection of Heaven and Earth. We are the antenna from which Universal Love is broadcast to the Earth. We are the eyes, ears, hands, and feet of the Universe. If we are on the right path, of the One True Source, that we make the right things happen. We create Harmony.

On "Giving Up" - September 26, 2010

Many individuals struggle with staying motivated and reaching their goals. For many people, the term "Giving Up" means simply to just quit or to admit defeat. At best, others consider the term to mean: "A verbal act of renouncing a claim or right or position". This idea does get closer, but there can be a deeper meaning of the term that the words themselves clearly say; even though many do not even notice it, being so caught up in tribulation. There is a surrendering or even a sacrificing implied in the term "give up", but if one examines and takes into consideration each of the two words of the term, one can receive much greater insight.

There is a definite "letting go" occurring when one "gives up", which brings us to the first word "Give". There is a reason that "give" is used. For when one finally surrenders after trying to use every manner of schemes and mechanizations to force to an outcome and finally "lets go" of one's grip, ONLY THEN can one lift this great burden and "Give" it away. With this letting go and giving, one finally gets a sense of relief. All the struggling and thinking and worrying and fighting and forcing and trying and failing all vanish once one finally stops and "gives". One finally 'abandons' this ceaseless struggle to force things to happen and there is a tremendous sense of relinquishing this hold to another who is more capable. Once one realizes just to "whom" one is relinquishing to, then it becomes clear that "giving up" does not have to be a negative emotional state, though it may have inadvertently proceeded it.

Which takes us to the second word: "Up". The use of the word "Up" for this term shows clearly that there is indeed a sense of direction for this giving, this abandoning and relinquishing of struggle and turmoil. Up implies a positive thing, a sense that there is movement going on above us, to a higher place, a higher calling, a higher energy, a higher vantage point than where we were struggling from. In "giving up" there is a gesture that is always done, where one lifts the arms and hands up towards the heavens. At this point, there is finally a letting go of this heavy weight, letting it be plucked from one's palms, immediately lightening the burdensome load. Indeed, success in reaching one's goal soon follows, strangely enough, when one finally "Gives Up". Hence, one is GIVING one's burdens UP to the heavens for relief. Soon enough, now calm of spirit, with nothing left that one can do anymore. There, the heavens (The One True Source / God / Goddess / Universe / Dao) can finally reach down and lift this burden off our hands, once we decide to stop trying to do things our way and we give God our trust to see things through.

So, when one understands the true nature of "Giving Up", one is far from being in a state of defeat but rather in a state of grace. Instead of struggle, we receive the light that illuminates our way because we are finally able to trust God to take care of our desires/wants/needs. For when we finally give up this stubbornness to do things our way and we let God as our creator take over, we then have our hands free to receive all the good that fulfills our lives. And, invariably, in this moment of truth, we receive not only peace but the answers we sought; often enough with even better results than we were trying for in the first place!

Here's what's happening when feeling strong emotions after practicing Qigong - October 2, 2010

New energy is coming into your system, while stale, worn out old energy is exiting your system. Your system stays in a state of harmony as long as what comes in and what goes out are equal. Where there's more input of new energy coming in and less going out of old energy, then your system goes into disharmony and it feels like chaos. But this is GOOD.

In this moment, you have two choices: to breakdown or to breakthrough. The fact that it is happening at all means that your capacity to handle things has INCREASED.

So, that means you can handle it, if you just breathe deep, slow down, and just enjoy what is happening right now. No thinking ahead or looking back. You are making a leap to a new level of achievement. You ARE able to breakthrough, you will feel much stronger and lighter and smarter and more energized and better.

You are already there, just accept it. The turmoil you feel is just the old world disappearing and the new world coming in to your awareness.

You already have more health, wealth, happiness, and prosperity. You have it now because your future self was created with these things when doing the Manifesting Qigong techniques. You just have to align your present physical self with your future spiritual self to get it. To do that, have to open your emotional blockages, so that your emotional center can open up and flow in harmony so that your physical and spirituals centers can unite.

Once you are open, giving and taking (sharing) can occur between yourself and the world around you. You can then let your sharing emotional self take care of things, give the world time to bring these things to you. The earth, your life, is now planted with the seed of your future self, so you have to accept that the seed is growing and developing in the earth and it is all coming to fruition.

There's nothing you have to do, it is a done deal. By being impatient and saying "I want it now!" you are stunting the growth of this new seed. Bamboo plants take 7 years to sprout from the seed! After that they grow in extreme abundance, one of the fastest grows plants known!

All you have to do is accept that you already have it, and LIVE LIKE IT IS ALREADY DONE. Increase your awareness that you have health, wealth, happiness, and prosperity. HOW it is going to happen is NOT YOUR CONCERN. Since it is a done deal, who cares? Just go on about your daily business with a new found awareness that you have these things in the making and they are yours and on their way to you, just like you ordered. It's not how you feel concerning your past, its how you carry your physical self now into your future, your higher self.

Weeping away is "always leaving, but never arriving". There is nothing to weep about, complete the past and squeeze it out. Choose what you want and take it.

Love Yourself First; the Rest will Follow - October 10, 2010

Qigong solves big problems in people's lives concerning health, wealth, happiness, and prosperity. Treating wellness by removing energy blockages helps people to overcome the pains associated with many illnesses, such as depression, anxiety, cancer, chronic fatigue, arthritis, osteoporosis, muscle soreness, and many more. As one of my teachers used to say: "How to do?". First is Alignment. Your physical self, which lacks, must go through your emotional center, which maybe be blocked and must be opened, to align with your spiritual self, which has all things already.

Alignment occurs on two levels:

1. Alignment with the Laws of Quantum Physics - In short, in the world of Quantum Physics - like thoughts (positive or negative) attract their equivalent or vibrational match. Whatever you focus on with intensity and emotion will set the Universe in motion to bring that into your life.

2. Conscious and Subconscious Alignment - Your Conscious desires and your Subconscious intention must be in alignment. If you Conscious Mind wants one thing and your Subconscious Mind wants something else (counter-intention) it is impossible to create what you want. It's that simple.

Once aligned and emotional blockages removed, then one is free to receive and transmit energy, which is manifesting or creating. It's Easy to Manifest Negativity! It takes work (Gong in Chinese) to manifest Positivity. You create more of whatever you have been focusing on. Whatever you are experiencing in your life right now is what you have been focusing on either consciously or unconsciously, no exceptions.

According to Dr. Robert Anthony (who was the original source of the information that inspired "The Secret" film) in his book *The Secret of Deliberate Creation*; "The real reason that you don't have what you want is because you are creating your life unconsciously by DEFAULT instead of consciously by DESIGN. Most of the time you are blocking the deliberate creation process because your conscious messages and your unconscious messages are in conflict. Through limited, mostly unconscious beliefs, and negative, unexamined habitual patterns, you are creating your life by DEFAULT. You cannot achieve success by simply slapping positive thoughts on top of a lifetime of negative expectations. You need to uncover and release the unconscious obstacles and habitual patterns that hold you back from creating the life you desire." In Qigong, all physical and mental disease is the manifestation of an emotional condition. Many people don't know how to manifest positive things in their life, but by default they know how to manifest negativity and illness. The failure to love one's self is at the root of nearly all physical problems.

In the book, *You Can Heal Your Life*, by Louise L. Hay, she explains that sooner or later, low self-esteem and the resulting lack of emotional health will translate into a breakdown of the body. This is most obvious with heart disease and cancer but likewise applies to other forms of illness. Withholding love for ourselves ages us prematurely. Our cells age and die and our bodies respond negatively from the deprivation of joy and happiness. We put on excess weight, develop ulcers, and are plagued by sickness and disease. Or, in an effort to numb our pain, we attempt to escape into the oblivion of drugs, alcohol, isolation or other addictions. In addition to this aspect of manifesting disease, when you don't love yourself, you don't treat yourself with respect. You live along the automatic assumption that you're not worth taking care of – eating right, exercising, getting medical attention, looking after your well-being. Disease results from what's going on at a cellular level, fueled by a deprivation of love.

According to Dr. Joe Rubino's *The Self Esteem Book*, "Loss of happiness, self-expression and vitality also stem from low self-esteem. Those lacking self-belief give up their ability to make a difference in others' lives. These costs spread to family members and afflict those closest to those lacking esteem. With the loss of happiness and self-expression comes loss of love, intimacy, partnership and affinity. It is difficult to love someone who does not love himself. Intimacy is a function of clean and open communication. Such communication is often the first casualty when self-esteem suffers."

What one postpones in dealing with in life comes back as pain. Some of this pain is found bound up within trigger points on the back, shoulders, arms, and legs. Once they are broken open and the negativity is released, one often suddenly remembers what the original emotional situation was that caused the blockage by being buried within. These memories are called "ghosts" in Qigong, and once they are released they are to be acknowledged but soon discarded to prevent their burial even deeper in the body. Once these "ghosts" become buried deeper, they begin to cause systemic dis-ease on the body, which effects one's emotional and spiritual centers as well. Removing emotional blockages in Qigong is the number one priority to restoring perfect health. Qigong does this through healing sessions, whereby a Qigong master not only removes layers of negative energy blockages but also go to the physical sites on the body where this bottled up negativity is located. By removing the blockages to harmonious energy flow through the energy streams (meridians) of your body, you are freed from negativity.

Once free of these blockages, Qigong lessons are often begun to maintain this new structural alignment. By learning qigong and practicing qigong - in effect you use qigong to heal yourself. In the long run, its not what's done to you, it's what you do to you.

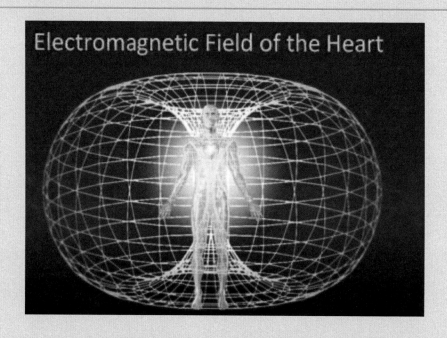

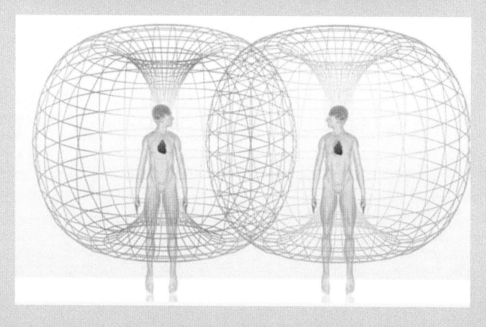

"Emotional fitness" Manifesting your Greatness - October 17, 2010

Qigong increases the level of circulation to the body, organs, glands, and nerves, which rejuvenates the body, mind, and spirit. Studies show that Qigong activates 90 percent of the brain. Qigong heals by raising energy levels high enough to push through blockages in the circulatory and nervous systems (like blowing through a straw to clear the path). A blockage is a small area where blood cannot fully go or where disease can occur. Qigong improves blood flow and opens blockages by relaxing the body so that your INTENTION can guide the blood through to closed off capillaries. Besides physical blockages (relationship with your body), there are also emotional (your relationship with others) and spiritual blockages (relationship with your higher self and the One True Source) as well. These are known as Unresolved Issues ("ghosts" as translated from the Chinese).

Avoiding discomfort (stress, tension, struggle, fear) is one of the major ways to create energy blockages: "Anything suppressed is expressed". What's worse is that 'stuff' that is avoided comes back instead as PAIN, major pain: "Pay attention or pay in pain". Says Robert Aitken Roshi in *The Gateless Barrier*: "If you try to cut off thoughts and feelings, thoughts and feelings will defeat your efforts and come flooding through, and you'll be desperately trying to plug the dike. Such an endeavor brings only despair. . . Notice and remember, notice and remember - a very simple, yet exacting practice."

According to Dr. Robert Anthony: "Struggle is trying to rearrange the world so that it aligns with the way you think it should be. It is the greatest source of unhappiness in our world today. It happens when you focus on what you perceive you don't have, instead of embracing what you do have. The denial or more accurately the resistance to your true nature is what keeps you struggling. Abundance is about lovingly accepting WHO and WHERE you are IN THIS MOMENT. It is focusing on all that you have and not losing yourself in all that you don't have. In the end, it is this thought that allows us to live in the Flow of unstoppable riches in every area of our lives." When you are in harmony with yourself and the universe (The One True Source), your spiritual, emotional, and physical centers no longer feel separate; free of blockages, they flow together until they form into one harmonious unit.

Also, according to Dr. Robert Anthony: "Another way to look at this is imagine the seed of the oak tree. Everything that defines the oak tree is already in the acorn. Unlike us, the acorn does not live under the illusion that it needs to be something else or needs to strive towards an accomplishment that is not in its nature. We are as great as we ALLOW ourselves to be. The problems is most of us don't ALLOW ourselves to live our greatness. Instead, we are quick to place huge limits on what we can do before we have even begun to do it. . . Today will bring you a new awareness, a lesson or a manifestation that you are making progress, no matter how large or small - IF YOU LOOK FOR IT! " The only limits you have are the ones you are placing on yourself. If you practice living in the "flow" and living in "alignment" your self imposed limits are unnecessary.

Qigong is a process by which one can direct one's Intention to specific ends, which increases Awareness, which in turn increases Attention. During Qigong practice you are constantly paying attention to HOW YOU THINK. Thoughts, Energy, and Intention work together. Qigong helps in GETTING PAST FEAR and "CONNECTING" ON A DEEP LEVEL. On a basic level, your own patterns of THINKING and FEELING lead to the ACTIONS you take and the BEHAVIOR you display. Negative feelings, more often than not, lead to NEGATIVE EMOTIONAL EXPERIENCES. If you are in CONTROL of your EMOTIONAL EXPERIENCES and have a handle on your own emotional state, then you can consistently create more POSITIVE EMOTIONAL EXPERIENCES.

Find something good that you can focus on. This is what will keep you in the "flow". You are out of the "flow" anytime you focus on or replay things in your mind that are not in alignment with the way you want to live. Focus (attention) on what you love. What you love shows in your results. Results are a mirror of what you pay attention to.

Program Your Mind to Turn Your Dreams and Desires Into Reality - October 24, 2010

One of the most basic skills of Qigong is being able to generate an energy flow through slow, graceful movements, coordinated with the breath. It is this energy flow that is vital to removing blockages to the harmonious flow of energy through the meridians (energy streams) of the body. Another basic skill of Qigong is meditation, which is being able to achieve stillness while directing the mind through the body to increase awareness. Both skills work in harmony (as a Yin / Yang relationship) to promote healing, purifying, and manifesting creative energy. When we harmoniously practice Stillness and Energy Flow, it is like we are cleaning dirt off a window and allowing the sunshine, WHICH HAS ALWAYS BEEN THERE, to flood through and light up your room. By requiring your mind to focus on specific actions in coordination with our breathing, we increase our awareness of our inner sensations and feelings. This increased awareness enhances our ability to pay attention to what we choose to at the moment, creating a meaningful flow of energy. When we have a meaningful flow of energy we have good health, vitality, and a long happy and prosperous life.

According to Dr. Robert Anthony: "Every action you take will either strengthen or weaken your power. Every time you give in to any impulse, your ability to resist it in the future becomes weaker. Anytime you are tempted by any behavior that is in contradiction to what you desire, you have a strengthening choice or a weakening choice. . . Say to yourself, "As I choose the strengthening decision now, I am making myself more powerful and my life easier from this moment on". As you practice this way of thinking every day, these decisions will become easier and easier because you will trust the "Flow", as a result, you will become more and more powerful by the minute.".

Thoughts and feelings are comprised of energy, how you harness this power creates your reality. During Qigong practice, when we shut off all the stressful and negative noise that over thinking brings on and instead focus on Joy and Gratitude, which is ultimately Giving and Receiving, we can be mindful of what good we already have now. The power of gratitude is very strong because it determines the outcome of our lives. This state of being allows us to grow more and more positive, and thus attracts to us more and more positive experiences. When we learn how to effectively shift how we think and behave in key situations, we take responsibility to creating the results we desire. Our Thoughts affect our Feelings, our Feelings effect our Actions, and the Actions we take effect the Results we get. By focusing your thoughts on joy and gratitude can have a powerfully positive effect on your feelings, which will affect the types of action you take and inevitably that will affect the results you get.

Increasingly, the field of Quantum Physics has shown what Qigong practitioners have known for 5,000 years: that your mind actually has the power to influence the creation of your external environment. It is like turning the radio dial to a station that plays music that uplifts and inspires us instead of listening to static noise that hurts us. Understand that WE are the antenna between Heaven and Earth, and so it is up to us to tune in the signals that are good for us, rather than waste our life on harmful noise. Whenever our mind starts to race with thoughts that bring us to nervousness, despair, anxiety, and so on, that is exactly when we must make the effort ('Gong' in Chinese) to "change the station" and list all the things that make us happy (regardless of what they are) and then all the things that we are grateful for. Allowing ourselves to feel Joy and Gratitude clears all the pains from our past, releasing us from condemning our future to be our past. We can complete the past and squeeze it out, by sitting still and knowing that we can choose a new vibrant life. The use of Qigong to heal your unresolved issues, purify your body, and to manifest what you desire allows you to regain Control Of Your LIFE and Achieve Your FULL POTENTIAL.

Everything Undulates - Understanding Neigong - November 1, 2010

In my Jindao system, there are three areas of benefit: 1) An integrated mind / body; 2) Peace of Mind; and 3) Self Transformation. One of the means used to achieve these results is Neigong. Neigong (neikung, neigung) means internal exercise or skill. Neigong includes qigong breathing exercises, loosening exercises (daoyin), and different forms of energy (jing) exercises. There is a great number of different exercises which cultivates the treasures of Jing (Essence), Qi (chi, energy, air, breath or life force) and Shen (Spirit) for health, longevity, and enlightenment. Neigong also is part of Chinese internal martial arts (neijia). Neigong is a vast system that connects such subjects as qigong, meditation, yoga, massage, healing, food therapy, and Traditional Chinese Medicine (TCM). The internal exercises of neigong also bring you happiness, peace, and enlightenment.

Neigong is a part of the 5,000 year old Daoist Neidan practice of internal alchemy in order to become a real or true human being, developed during an era when those who were wise were very closely connected with Nature and themselves. At that time, one was considered healthy when one lived in unity with the cosmos, and ill when one subdued one's own emotions. The true human being is beyond the desires of the dissatisfied spirit. Neigong in essence is transformation techniques, which are aimed at living as one with the vast, unfathomable energy of Nature. The mother of all learning processes for a Daoist is Nature. Through observation one realizes that there are no straight lines in Nature, only curves, waves, and spirals. There is only flow: fluidity without rigidity; firmness without flaccidness. Everything undulates. Thus, the spontaneous naturalness of life – everywhere and in every form – is the fundamental principle of a Daoist.

Daoist life practices include not only medicine and martial arts, but also the systems of transformation, which cover all areas of life – the arts of changing resonance, vibrations. Daoist philosophic texts could help to convey such knowledge from teacher to student, but only to the extent that the trainee is prepared to explore Nature and the further development of the teachings prompted by one's own creative motivation. Becoming a neigong master meant that you would have a lifetime of research. Commitment to the Dao (The Way, the One True Source) meant commitment to Creation.

Following this path of perfecting existence involves the training of your individual perception. When doing the Neigong movements you are told to "Relax into your own being". The Daoist learns from the embryo of a human being or from a sleeping animal, such as a cat or snake, to store energy at the center of a coiling spiral in a restful or sleeping position, or to preserve the energy of life in this position. In this way, you can feel the breath of the cosmos (energetic vibrations made out of light), which is known as Qi.

Three types of Qi are distinguished in the human being. The first is the prenatal Qi, which is produced from our genetic code (Jing) and gives our body its individual characteristics. In the second, we have the "acquired" Qi, the life energy, which we develop by eating and breathing. The third is the etheric Qi, which we produce through our thought and concentration potential. Qi is a term for the etheric life energy which contains life-giving light in various frequencies. The authentic teachings make it possible for the adept to synchronize the three circles of human vitality and thereby to harmonize them, thus enabling sheer vitality to unfold.

When the female aspect is united with the masculine, the great art of flow, of circulating energy, is attained. This universal Qi created order and energy, which allows all things to exist. Look at the sky and you will see your inner space. Look into your inner space – and you will discover the sky. Just as you were once inside your mother's womb, so too today are you always within the womb of the cosmos. Inside this womb, we are all of one source. From our cells to the stars everything is connected and in constant communication. All things are being experienced at all times. There is no "good" or "bad", there just IS. Inside your mother's womb you were breathing in water; similarly today you are breathing in the Qi of the cosmos.

Thus, we are permeated and surrounded by various forms of vibrations, whether we like it or not. Dealing with these vibrations – channeling, concentrating, and bringing them into a natural balance – is what the term "gong" conveys: more simply described as "work" or more elegantly as "unfolding". The primary factors in the Daoist teachings of transformation are: storing, directing, regulating, and refining life energy. If Qi were defined as the universal energy, there would preferably be two fundamental characteristics to emphasize: tangible and intangible energy. Objects that you can see are made of tangible energy. Since Thoughts are made of intangible energy, they are things as well, once formed they have an energy of their own that effects everything that one directs attention to. Modern quantum physics is gradually converging with the ancient knowledge of the alchemical magician: Light is "creative", the cosmos is unpredictably magical change. Therefore, the creative human being is capable of producing the most Qi. Perfect tone, poetry, color, light, and vibrations, find your elemental personal expression of creation and perfect your Being through perfecting the arts.

Positive Thinking on it OWN is not Enough - November 7, 2010

A famous saying in metaphysics is "As above, so below". What is happening within the body is a clue to what issues are affecting someone's life outside of the physical body. When there is stagnation, obstruction, or depletion of energy or Qi in any one area there is a domino effect that will eventually cause other symptoms to occur both physically or environmentally. Treating symptoms in isolation will not necessarily affect a cure, since the underlying energetic cause of the problem may lie in areas other than where the symptom occurred.

Hilda Wei Williams, a Chinese Qigong master, says, "A winning attitude, positive thinking, and intent and visualization — these are all great tools that can drive us to succeed, but are these enough? . . . Put your positive attitude to work for you. Don't just ask — go out and look for it! Write your future, fulfill your dreams, and make your destiny! . . . you get as much as you put in . . . You decide how much time and effort your success is worth . . . Success comes from more than positive thinking but also hard work. . . Don't have the time? Make time. Don't have the knowledge? Go educate yourself! . . . Qigong is no different. If you want to master the art of qigong, you have to be willing to put in the practice. Positive thinking and yinian or the yi mind power are the keys to controlling the Qi, your intrinsic lifeforce, but without sufficient training and practice, you still have no *Qi* to control."

Qi permeates everything and links the parts of our surroundings together. Once you are a master of your Qi, your life force, then you can move beyond that to create your own manifestation.

To illustrate: Many people watched the film, The Secret and came away from it with a great sense of hope. But then they grew increasingly frustrated and even angry that despite all their inspired motivation, nothing much actually happened different in their lives. This sad situation was a result of confusing the fantasy of "things getting better" with the real WORK deliberately creating new energy. There are various factors involved doing energy work, which include motivation, positive thinking, integrated mind / body, resolution, strong effort, and intent. But, ALL these factors are necessary to achieve real results. Positive thinking is all well and good, but it won't get rid of your obstacles for you.

Sales and motivation speaker Zig Ziglar tells this relevant story:

"A very wealthy man wanted to see who was worthy enough to marry his only daughter, so he invited all of his daughter's suitors to his large real estate. All of his property and wealth, he said, would go to the man who married his daughter, if he could pass one test, and that was to swim across an alligator-infested lake.

Well, for the longest period of time, there was silence, as no one wanted to put his life on the line. Suddenly, without a word, one man jumps into the lake and begins to swim as fast as he could, with the alligators snapping close behind him. When he finally reaches the other side, he is huffing with exertion, but fortunately in one piece. His prospective father-in-law rushes to his side congratulating him on his success and having won his daughter's hand in marriage. What, he asked, did the young man have to say to that?

Still breathing hard from his exertions, the young man said, "Just one thing…who pushed me in?!"

Says Zig: "Positive thinking didn't play a major role here. This man was motivated because he had no choice …but look how his motivation *pushed* him to succeed! What winning attitude can drive you to succeed? What mountain of obstacles do you have to cross that will make your success all that much sweeter?"

Do You Know Your True Heart's Desire? - November 21, 2010

No matter what we do, no matter how much we try to hide it, people are simply NOT happy when they are not following their true heart's desire. Doing what they are forced to do by circumstance, biology, making other people happy at the expense of our own happiness, working for people or companies that do not appreciate us, or simply not even KNOWING what our heart's desire is yet brings people to a state of apathy, despair, or anxiety. Following our heart's desire brings us a sense of purpose that nothing else can satisfy. Some people try to bury this feeling with drinking, drugs or other vices, but deep down the feeling of un-satisfaction is not only still there but grows even stronger.

Since everything is made of energy, everything in our life vibrates, including our thoughts, ideas, and emotions. When our actions match our current feelings, our bodies physically, emotionally, and spiritually resonate in unison. Even the latest issues of Scientific American and Science magazines discuss studies that show that a "wandering mind is an unhappy one", where the latest research shows that being absorbed in what you do makes us feel more fulfilled. Our most fulfilling experiences are typically those that fully engage us body and mind; during these moments we feel free of worry or regret. Instead, we feel recharged and vital. Fulfilling pursuits ("following our heart's desire") keep us focused. When our attention is deeply absorbed in doing what make's us happy, we find that we attract even more of the positive things or experiences in our lives that continue to fulfill us.

On the other hand, doing what we don't really want to do makes our mind wander. When we are not doing what makes us happy, since our attention is focused on unpleasant actions, we get not only negative feeling but also negative results. Just like the wise traditions teach, we're happiest when thought and action are aligned, even if they're only aligned to wash dishes. When we do what we don't really want to do, our minds start to wander and then begin to feel unhappy. Mental presence - the matching of thought to action - is a strong predictor of happiness.

The problems with happiness start when you are out of control. You walk around in a dream, pretending you're awake, pretending you're in control of your life. But you're not. Your mind or your body is in control, but not "You". You walk around pretending you are in control, but instead mental programs that you are often not even aware of block you from being true to yourself. They're pulling the strings behind the scenes - and most of the time we're NOT EVEN AWARE OF IT. What's in control is our habit patterns, our habitual emotions, our drives, our past experiences, etc., all of which act as blockages that stagnate. But if we want to move forward with our lives, if we want to transform, we must remove these blockages and then manifest our true purpose.

Says motivation expert Steven G. Jones, "Realize this, everything that you want out of life, you want because you feel it brings you happiness. Be it wealth, health, relationships, love, abundance or anything else, the reason why you desire these things is because they represent happiness to you. The other reason you may make a decision or desire something is to avoid consequence or pain. If you feed your subconscious thoughts of what represents pain or consequence and constantly make decisions to avoid those things, you will spend your life achieving your objectives but never gaining true happiness."

Says Dr. Robert Anthony, "The only time we suffer is when we believe a thought that argues with "what is". When the mind is perfectly clear, "what is" is what we accept in this moment. People should be... My neighbors should be... My husband should... My wife should... I should. These thoughts are ways of wanting reality to be different than it is. Here is my point - all the stress you feel in your life at this moment is caused by arguing with "what is". Accepting "what is" doesn't mean you condone or approve of the way things are, it just means you give up all the resistance and inner struggle by wishing it were different. No one wants to lose their money, have their children get sick or be in a car accident. However, when these things happen it can be helpful not to mentally argue with them. We know better than to do that, yet we do it because it is a HABITUAL PATTERN . . . It is simple logic. Before the thought you were not suffering. With the thought you are suffering. When you recognize the thought isn't true, you will go back to not suffering and return to happiness."

Continues Dr. Robert Anthony, "Living in the Flow and living in abundance is about focusing on WHO YOU ARE and what you can do in this moment. It is not about who you are not, what you cannot do, and what you don't have. WHO YOU ARE is everything. It is the ONLY thing that really matters because everything hinges on your ability to be yourself and to do that you must become intimately aware of the false beliefs you have about yourself and about the way life works. Who we are is our True and Authentic Self that is always connected and one with Source Energy. On the other hand, who we THINK we are is how we show up in life. If we are struggling we will never be who we are. Who we THINK we are comes from listening to other people rather than listening to ourselves."

So, how do you find out what is your heart's desire? When you quiet the inner dialogue in your head and free your true and authentic self to finally hear what is deep in your soul, THEN you will feel what is right for you. The good news is that the practice of Qigong trains our heart and our mind to unite as one (called the Yi in Chinese, which translates as "intention"). Qigong teaches us how to generate energy from inside our bodies with our mind. This ability allows us to transform our selves so that we do and think at the same time, achieving greater mental presence, which makes us feel happier since we are not conflicted between what we are doing and what we are thinking. We have control over our thoughts and our bodies. With regular and dedicated Qigong meditative practice, we can become much more present, mindful, and content. From that state of grace, you are able to transform your feelings and take back control of your life so that you are free to do what your true heart desires.

A Life of Trust - December 5, 2010

According to the great philosopher of the 1600s, Baruch Spinoza, when we are confused or we lack understanding, we feel pain and we desperately require the feeling and the sense that we need power. But, if we want power we have to get our self-approval from outside of us, not within us. This sense that we need more power to get things to happen is the very thing that separates us from being one with the flow of nature because it forces us to struggle. Struggling to "make" things happen is an unconscious habitual pattern. Most habits or patterns are learned early in our life. Habits are learned and repeated and are a part of who we believe we are.

In Andrew Perry's article, *A Guide to Understanding Spinoza's Ethics*, he says that "According to Spinoza's philosophy, people are guided by reasons, and people who have habits ("mental addictions") have reasons for their behavior (though they are not always aware of them). As Spinoza suggested more than 300 years ago, it is this mental addiction, or "desire," that is the source of people's behavior. Even if a person really wanted to do something different, they couldn't because they will always act according to their desires. That's why so many smokers who quit wind up smoking again, even after many years of abstinence. In order to stop smoking, Spinoza would suggest paying attention to those particular instances that cause one to smoke. This awareness will bring to light the reasons one has for smoking. Then, the smoker needs to evaluate the reasons and see if they are actually good reasons. Smokers should also think about the reasons they had to begin smoking. Are the reasons still applicable today? In reviewing all the reasons, one lessens the desire. By becoming knowledgeable about the reasons for their desire, Spinoza says that a person becomes wise, and wisdom will cause a person to alter his bad behavior. This is done basically by switching masters, instead of physical vice, wisdom becomes the master. It would be inaccurate to refer to this process as "quitting smoking". Quitting requires effort of will. Spinoza would probably add that since the smoker no longer has the desire to smoke, the smoker's behavior has followed suit. The ex-smoker isn't doing anything; the only difference is that he's not smoking."

Continues Perry in his article, "By acquiring knowledge, Spinoza talks about a "meditation of life", becoming aware of one's life and the reasons he may have for behaving in certain ways. Bad behavior is almost always guided by faulty reasoning due to desires, and good behavior is guided by good reasons. Spinoza says that this conscious attention toward life will bare the reasons humans have for behaving in certain ways. Bad reasons will fall away, and with those so too will the desire. With wisdom as the person's new master, the person will no longer be satisfied by simple physical desires. Instead, the person will begin to seek knowledge and even the greater good, and this pursuit will satisfy the person instead."

Within Taoism there is a strong tenet to be at one with nature, which implies trusting that you do not need to struggle to meet your goals. Everything that has been created in the Universe (The Dao or Tao) has its own natural flow that requires no struggle when it operates. Thus, says Dr. Robert Anthony: "Water does not struggle to flow. Grass does not struggle to grow. Wind does not struggle to blow. Rain does not struggle to fall. Sun does not struggle to shine. Earth does not struggle to rotate. Flowers do not struggle to bloom. . . Awareness is the first step to making any change in our lives. If you are aware that struggle is not "normal" and that it is a learned UNCONSCIOUS HABITUAL PATTERN, you can CONSCIOUSLY make the choice not to live your life paddling upstream."

In fact, by "going with the flow", you don't "have" to do anything. Once you make your desires known to Nature, and trust that your desires will be met, everything falls into place in its own due time. You will be inspired to be at the right place at the right time, and know when to do what. As long as you don't just sit at home waiting for things to happen and instead go out and interact with people, then the correct path will be revealed. This is called "inspired action", in that inspiration leads our intuition to feel which way to go so that the best results can be achieved. Our feelings act as a guidance system. As long as we are on the correct path, we feel good. Once we leave the path, either by doing something we shouldn't or not doing something we should, then we feel like we are struggling. We become uneasy, nervous, anxious, unhappy, confused, agitated, or lost. We feel wrong on the inside. On the outside our struggling also allows negative emotions, as they show themselves to others, to become active and public.

Sometimes, however, these emotions become frozen and are held deep within us, often unconsciously. Our emotions then go out of balance, and we become cluttered with emotional baggage which upsets our lives, often for many years. Unreleased emotions keep haunting you, and the Chinese even call these "Ghosts". This blockage may be felt as tension, pain, or heat. When an energy blockage is held within, it creates suffering whether it is emotional or physical pain. Holding energy blocks the flow of energy, just like a dam or snags in a river and it stops the in-coming flow of new energy - it creates a lack. This lack can be in any form: love, money, time, happiness, comfort, success, and health. There is no room for anything else to enter and you stay stagnant. Nothing can come in when there is nothing going out. Once a blockage is formed, energy cannot flow freely in our energy channels. These energy channels run throughout the body to keep it fully functioning. Energy is dynamic, it is always moving, flowing, changing, magnetic, and its vibration frequency is expansive. Dammed up energy accumulates, which starts moving again after removing the blockage. Energy always seeks constant flow through release. The practice of Qigong meditation and energy healing allows you to unblock these negative emotions. Qigong Tui Na Energy Healing is a special branch of Chinese medicine designed to unblock, free, and balance qi in others. Qigong healing relates to energy points in your body and to the manipulation of those points to positively affect your emotions, tension, and physical condition. Qigong is designed to relax the mind and body and help unblock stress and tension. Also, the practice of Qigong allows you to replace negative habits or behaviors with positive ones.

Sprouting Seeds in Your Garden - December 12, 2010

Many spiritual traditions say "As above, so below". Above all, Qigong is an Alchemical process, a method of transforming the self from a lower form to a higher form, much like a tiny seed germinates and grows to be a tree or plant. Germination is the process in which a plant or fungus emerges from a seed or spore and begins growth. Also, germination can imply anything expanding into greater being from a small existence. Most seeds go through a period of quiescence where there is no active growth; during this time the seed can be safely transported to a new location and/or survive adverse climate conditions until circumstances are favorable for growth. Quiescent seeds are ripe seeds that do not germinate because they are subject to external environmental conditions that prevent the initiation of metabolic processes and cell growth. In nature, some seeds require particular conditions to germinate, such as the heat of a fire, or soaking in a body of water for a long period of time. Qigong theory states that physical transformation of the body needs to occur to bring your inner soul or Higher Self in harmony with the universal soul or One True Source. Qigong is part of the process of PREPARING your body, heart, and spirit so that your desires, or spiritual seeds, can come into fruition.

A farmer or gardener plants seeds under the proper conditions, adds water, and walks away. How or why that seed will germinate is not his concern. He just lets nature do its work. On a spiritual level, people plant seeds all the time. Every desire you have is a seed seeking to germinate and come to fruition. But, do you pull up the seeds planted in your garden to see if they are growing yet? By doubting or worrying, that's exactly what you are doing! You are telling the seeds that you demand them to show you results right now. That's a sure fire way to not only stop the growth, but also in killing the seed itself. Impatience, one of your worst enemies! By focusing on the ABSENCE of physical proof (what you don't have or don't want), you are slowing or halting the very thing that you desire to come into being. How that seed is going to germinate is not your problem, the Universe or the True Source (the Dao / Tao) working with your Higher Self will take care of that. But do you trust your Higher Self or the One True Source or do you keep looking for evidence that they are "doing something"? Just because you don't see your desires met in physical reality at the moment, doesn't mean they are not on the way to you. 99% of the creative work of something coming into being (seeds sprouting), happens BEFORE you ever see anything. Seeds look dormant but they are not; they are using energy that is the equivalent of a bursting megabomb from the moment it is planted to the moment they finally sprout.

Just like seeds need to soak up water before cellular metabolism and growth can resume because they are dry inside, so too does Qigong provide the life force of the universe -- Qi (Chi) -- to soak inside our bodies to counteract the stagnation of our heart and spirit. Just like Oxygen is required by the germinating seed for metabolism, so too does Qigong's breathing methods bring Oxygen deep into the body to give it internal energy. Just like temperature affects the cellular and metabolic growth rate of germination, so too does Qigong's healing methods warm or cool off your body as needed. Just like many seeds will not sprout unless there is sufficient light for growth of the seedling, so too does Qigong's meditation methods provide the light necessary for peace of mind. Finally, after all the necessary factors for new life to spring forth from the seed and grow strong and bear fruit, so too does Qigong's Healing, Purifying, and Manifesting methods provide you with all the best things for the physical, emotional, and spiritual transformation necessary for your desires to come to fruition.

Scientific Proof that 'Our thoughts create our reality' - January 2, 2010

Thoughts lead to emotions or feelings that often manifest as physical symptoms and habitual behavior. People that work in the Healing Arts know this, but there exists scientific medical proof for this idea.

According to medical science (from the article "*Neuropeptides: the molecules of emotions*" by Dr Arien van der Merwe): "Peptides consist of strings of amino acids of varying lengths, joined together in a necklace by very strong bonds made of carbon and nitrogen. Between 10 and 100 amino acids that form a strong bond, are called peptides. Amino acids are the letters that when combined in certain sequences, form the words that are peptides, or the sentences that are polypeptides or proteins. These all make up a language that forms and directs the function of every single cell, organ and system inside the body, from the deepest vibrations of the DNA molecule inside the nucleus of every cell, to the macrocosmic systems function of the whole individual being. Common peptides include the endorphins (our own happy hormones), insulin (responsible for blood sugar control), vasopressin (responsible for blood pressure), sex hormone releasing hormones, serotonin (the feel-good neurotransmitter)."

Peptides are made not only in the body but in the brain as well, which makes neuropeptides. Well known groups of neuropeptides include the neurotransmitters that carry messages across synapses in the nervous system, growth factors, gut peptides, immune system modulators (e.g., growth inhibitors that tell cells when to stop growing). A better term for the peptides might be *informational substances*. They form a two-way network between the mind and body. Dr. Candace Pert is a neuroscientist who did a lot of research on the neuropeptides (http://www.candacepert.com/). She was the first to call them the 'molecules of emotions' in her books. More than 90 neuropeptides have been identified so far, associated with mood changes, nerve, hormone, and immune regulation.

One of the revolutionary findings that Candace Pert discusses is that body chemicals form an information network that links the body and mind. According to Candace Pert's research: Depending on the thoughts and emotions, specific neuropeptides are made in the brain and nervous system, white blood cells, reproductive system, digestive system and heart, and more. All the neuropeptides have a similar molecular structure, with subtle differences in the tertiary structure, meaning that only the frequency and amplitude at which each molecule oscillates (wavelike vibrations of electrons in each molecule), differ. Neuropeptides change configuration (like a chameleon) due to emotional influence, according to specific thoughts and emotions. Dr. Pert has explained in popular lectures throughout the world how emotions exist both as energy and matter, in the vibrating receptors on every cell in the body. She describes the mysterious energy connecting body to mind & emotions as the free flow of information carried by the biochemical of emotion: neuropeptides and their receptors.

Says Dr. Pert, "The fact that the word "trauma" has been used to describe both physical and mental damage has been a key part of my theory of how the molecules of emotion integrate what we feel at every level of what I've called our bodymind. As a practical manner, people have a hard time discriminating between physical and mental pain. So often we are "stuck" in an unpleasant emotional event – a trauma – from the past that is stored at every level of our nervous system and even on the cellular level – i.e., cells that are constantly becoming and renewing the nervous system. My laboratory research has suggested that all of the senses, sight, sound, smell, taste and touch are filtered, and memories stored, through the molecules of emotions, mostly the neuropeptides and their receptors, at every level of the bodymind."

She explains and demonstrates how the brain, immune system, and endocrine system link and communicate with each other. For example, Neuropeptides cause chemical changes in the body that can improve or weaken the immune system. Stress and depression can suppress the activity of lymphocytes, the white blood cells that are the body's first line of defense against cancer and invading organisms. Diseases of the immune system include HIV/aids, cancer, allergies, arthritis, infections, the auto-immune disorders such as ulcerative colitis, multiple sclerosis and rheumatoid arthritis, and many other conditions that are a consequence of either a under-

or an over-active immune system. Cells in the immune system are responsive to all 90 neuropeptides that are triggered by our thoughts and emotions. When people raise their self esteem, it has been shown that their immune systems get boosted as well.

Another example: according to Dr. Arien's article, "The specific feel-good peptide (e.g. serotonin), bind to its specific receptors on the cell membrane. This sends a 'feel-good' message to the inside of the cell, right into the nucleus. The message influences every function the cell is responsible for. Now consider the fact that you constantly think of things others have done to harm you; resentful, angry thoughts and feelings that grow and increase to disproportionate levels every time you think it. The thoughts become emotions, then the neuropeptides that course through your body-mind, influencing cell function and efficacy. Do you think that any cell receiving these messages for 30 years, would still feel like functioning well enough for you to be optimally happy, alive and fully self-actualizing to become all you're meant to be?" Now THAT is food for thought! In the same way we can get addicted to drugs because we have receptors for these drugs we can become addicted to emotions; with molecules of emotions, like anger, worrying, or depression, we get addicted to the emotion and we act out the same patterns over and over again. There patterns block us from changing and force us to suffer with habitual behaviors that stagnate our growth.

Continues Dr. Arien: "Your cells *feel* the way you do! Your thoughts *do* create your reality! What you spend your time thinking about, becomes the facts of your life. That's why positive affirmations actually work – repeating simple, positive, powerful statements to yourself, changes the frequency of the vibrations around your own neuropeptides, allowing cells to function better, your mind to find solutions to reach your goals, and your whole body-mind system to function optimally. Changing your habitual thought patterns to one of positivity and love, such as ' I am calm in my body, in my mind and in my emotions', 'I succeed', 'I feel calmness flowing through me', 'I love, accept and approve of myself just as I am', 'I live my truth', 'let go let God', or the Sanskrit mantra, 'om gum gana patayei namaha' to remove energy blockages, will allow the electrons around the nucleus of your neuropeptides to send positive, feel-good vibrations of waves and particles throughout your body-mind being. These vibrations bind to your cell receptors and allow the message to go right into your physical and spiritual DNA, the genetic source of your being. . . Emotions like bitterness, unresolved anger, resentment, fear and worry constantly trigger your stress response. These then become buried in ever deepening layers inside the cell memories. The layers become the physical footprints of your dream body, psyche or soul, manifesting in physical illness or chronic health problems."

Concludes Dr. Arien: "Where are your thoughts? Anticipation, fear and worry are mostly in the future where you have no control. Unresolved anger, bitterness, resentment are in the past. You can only learn, grow and let go of the past. You can never change it. So why waste your precious life force energy there? These thoughts prevent you from being in the present, the NOW, which is all you have. Thoughts lead to emotions or feelings that often manifest as physical symptoms and habitual behavior."

In the Jindao Qigong healing system that I practice, during the Shaolin Pre-Natal Qigong method, the true source of pain or illness is revealed. This revelation awakens buried memories that serve as blockages within the body and mind. These blockages cause stagnation, which are expressed as pain and illness. Once the cell memories are wakened, they can reach the conscious mind, so that you can make contact with your whole, integrated human *beingness,* leading to the identification of the deep issues that might play a role in the disease process. Healing is fast and immediate at this point. Through this, pain or disease becomes a teacher potentially leading to important life lessons, personal and spiritual growth and healing from the inside out. Many people who have experienced Qigong energy healing from me can indeed attest to this very thing happening before their pains and illnesses were released for good.

Also, in the Jindao Qigong healing system, during healing, purifying, and manifesting, one is told to create the thoughts about what one desires on a spiritual level and then one vibrates their physical self to merge with this spiritual self by intentionally causing one's emotional center to feel the emotions of Joy and Gratitude. These very powerful emotions (E-Motion, energy in motion, which is the literal definition of the Chinese words "Qi Gong"), it can be seen through the research of Candace Pert, create positive vibrations that ring like a bell throughout one's body and soul. Thoughts are things, not only in concept, but also as real physical molecules that are produced and change one's life, positively or negatively. As Dr. Robert Anthony says "When suffering becomes worse than change, you will change"! The great news is that not only is the Choice yours but you have the real ability to create this change, break your addiction to negative emotions, and release yourself from suffering because you can completely recover by choosing your thoughts and creating a new vision for yourself and basically a new brain.

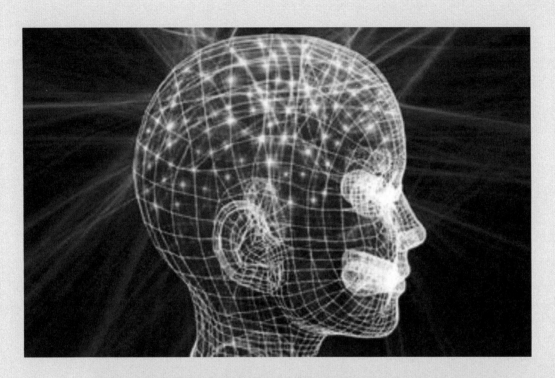

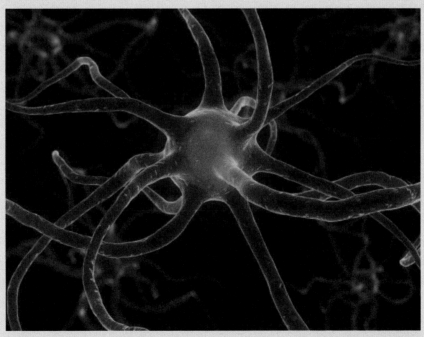

What you want already exists right now, not outside of you but within you - January 16, 2011

Manifestation is a topic of concern for many people today, primarily because most people are now looking to better their lives in some way or other. People see that I list Manifesting as part of the Jindao Health Transforming Qigong system that I practice and teach. They ask me what manifesting has to do with Qigong and healing and purifying. Well, Qigong is a way of making internal transformations happen that create external manifestations. The definition of 'manifesting' is "to make something apparent", also to "clearly reveal something to the mind, the senses, or to the judgment". Meaning, a creative act ("to make") or a process ("reveal") was performed so that "something was understood" or "something happened" or "something was made" to create a change or transformation inside you that now shows itself outside you. Thus, when you manifest a thing or event (health or wealth or whatever) you reveal it or make it apparent not only to yourself but to others. So, Manifesting IS when you show the results of creating a change or transformation.

This internal transformation is a creative act because it MAKES results (which means that health, wealth, prosperity, etc., are actually the results of performing a process or a creative act). Furthermore, t he creative act itself can be seen as the process of manifesting the union of our Imagination and our Intent. Imagination + Intent = Manifestation. Both Imagination and Intent involve using the mind and body to perform a creative act. Imagination is the internal creation of an image, thought, or idea. Intent is the internal creation of a purposeful desire to act. Intent is pure spirit in motion. Imagination can be so vivid that people actually generate strong feelings in their bodies when they think of the images they are creating in their mind. Intentions can be so focused that people generate strong feelings in their bodies when they think of the desires they are creating in their mind. Thus, Imagination involves thinking about being / doing and Intent involves doing what you are thinking about. When we align Imagination with Intent, we are able to achieve strong results. People imagine things all the time that never materialize, but when Intent is added to Imagination, what we intently and purposefully focus on becomes real because it already feels real (before we see it materialize). You feel it into reality. In the Qigong system, if the results that you don't want are happening, they are happening unconsciously, and they are trying to reveal something that is stuck in your energetic pathways. When we don't align Imagination with Intent, we can manifest what we don't want equally with what we do want. Or, we manifest random results that either stagnate or hurt us in the long run.

People naturally manifest all the time. For example, when writing, people's imagination clearly merges with their intentions and the hand transmits this in the form of writing. Likewise, people manifest when they draw, paint, sculpt, compose a song or photo, and so on. During these acts, people often BEGIN with the END result already in mind. They have this final image clearly available to themselves so that they can then EXPRESS this preconceived image (as a drawing, as a painting, as a sculpture, as a photo, as a book, as a song, as a dance, and so on). The act of expression (Intent) then is the bridge from Imagination to the final manifestation. Neville once wrote and shared, "A change in your feeling is a change in your destiny". Manifestation then is when people create results (things or events). For example, an internal transformation happens through Qigong methods that exhibits itself as a thing or event (makes a result), such as Health. Wealth is just social health. Prosperity is just financial health. To manifest this result, people begin with Health (the end result) in mind, not with disease in mind. They perform actions that express their intention to be healthy and feel their final image of themselves as being healthy. Health then is a manifestation of what you are thinking and doing and feeling, such as eating right, taking supplements, detoxifying the body, practicing Qigong, transforming the self through meditation and a positive attitude, and so on.

Mind, body, and spirit are all really the same thing. There is no use to separate them, as it implies we are divided against ourselves. Since EVERYTHING is made of Energy, everything is really Spirit, Pure Source, all really one whole person. Qigong, because it includes Manifesting as well as Purifying, goes beyond mere healing but rather allows for Self Transformation to happen. Healing implies that there is disease, which just makes a state where we are expecting this negativity to be there, testing and treating negativity. Instead,

Transforming is going outside our current state, releasing our negative expectations, and choosing a positive alternative. The energy to choose change is inside us all, we just guide people to this awareness. Once enlightened, we are freed of any negative expectations, releasing pain, blocked emotions, stagnant energy, and so on. Says Paul Bauer about Manifesting, "Imagine what your life would be like if you were to choose to live from your Heart and in the trust that what you desire is already real . . . the essence of creation is *aligning with what you want being real **right now** -- feeling it, **breathing into it** and feeling the essence of it being here right now and **being grateful** for that.*"

You already are that which you seek - January 23, 2011

Previously I wrote about Manifesting and how it arises from combining emotionally felt Imagination with heart felt Intention. According to Paul Bauer, "Intent is pure energy. It's pure spirit in motion. Every thought, every feeling you feel is intent. Therefore, you're always intending. Each time you think or feel, you're placing attention on something. In other words, you're giving it energy (positive or negative). As you begin to notice what's "showing up" in your life, you then begin to see the effects of your intent in motion."

Results come when you feel that your desires are already real. But one thing that has to be made perfectly clear is that "manifesting" is not about forcing things to happen. It is not about doing 'magic spells' that instantly create new stuff for you to have. It's really about GETTING OUT OF YOUR OWN WAY SO THAT WHAT IS BEST FOR YOU CAN COME ABOUT. This idea means that you are ACTIVE with your INTENT so that you can MANIFEST what you really NEED versus what you think you WANT. One has to understand that manifesting is not about striving for or trying to "attract" but rather LETTING WHAT YOU ALREADY HAVE INSIDE YOU FREE TO COME INTO BEING.

What is "inside" us? First, one must understand what we are made of. In Qigong, the Dao (Tao) is a name for the one true Source of all that exists. People call this Source many things: God, Goddess, Great Spirit, etc. Scientists, especially physicists, agree that 'Everything that exists in the Universe came from ONE Source that made it all come into being'. Most spiritual traditions of all types will say just about the same thing. Furthermore, everything that exists has some kind of Energy (the measurable ability to produce physical changes) and Energy not only vibrates, has different frequencies, but it also transforms from one form into another form. In Qigong, Energy is called 'Universal Qi' and is a living force. Nikola Tesla said, "If you wish to understand the secrets of the Universe, think of energy, frequency, and vibration." Energy, frequencies, sounds, and vibrations are all around us, even if you can not hear, see, or sense them in any way AND they are always affecting us.

Since everything is made of this creative Source energy, we can never be separate from this Source, neither can our energy. We thus are Source energy. Albert Einstein said that "A human being is part of the whole, called by us the "Universe" – a part limited in time and space. He experiences himself, his thoughts and feelings as something separate from the rest – a kind of optical delusion of consciousness. " In ultimate reality there is only one thing and that's Life. It all starts with Being (we are individually a part of the Whole creation) and the Power within. We are everything, we are all that is. The fact is that WE are pure Source, not separated from it by any law.

Many people believe that the premise of the "law of attraction" is that if you "do" something - and do it the "right way", then you'll "attract" something, as if it is a pipe that can be tapped into. But what is false about this premise is that it implies that you are separate from the very thing your mind thinks you need to "attract". In other words, why if you are Source would you need to attract anything at all? The flaw is that every time you think you need to attract something (or align, do, shift vibration, etc.) you actually send the signal to your subconscious mind that you don't have it to begin with. And that signal is your feelings. Feelings always are more powerful than thoughts. So your consistent thoughts and their resultant feelings will eventually manifest themselves as the results of your life - good or bad.

Thus, you get what you think about, whether you like it or not, so you must watch where you put your attention to. Otherwise, you condemn your future to be your past. When you change the way you look at things, the things you look at will change. You are bringing the future into the present. Again according to Paul Bauer: "Tuning into the feeling of *already having it* is the key. For the sheer joy of feeling it. Regardless of whether it shows up or not. Yes - you read right... That's when it becomes pure intent - when you decide that the feeling is the key and all that's really important is the Essence of your intent. Not how it shows up in the physical world (or "when"). When you choose to feel the Essence of your intent already being real, your intent purifies."

When you finally understand that "I have within me all that I need and desire", your "field of awareness" opens up so that things, events, ideas, people, possibilities, wealth, prosperity, health, and so on will begin to "show up" in your field of vision and your daily life. According to the study of quantum physics and qigong, there is no need to 'attract' anything at all. When we intend to change our life and manifest what we desire – we are allowing ourselves to 'see' what is already there.

Once you stop trying so hard, and just "be", and, once you let go of "wanting", then, everything falls into place and the Universe unfolds just as it should. Thus, "not enough" (lacking, wanting, needing) is an illusion caused by the illusion of 'separation' that Einstein spoke of. This myth about attracting something from the outside to you is old separation consciousness. The new paradigm for the 21st century is not about how much you can get or have. It's about how you can contribute – and the universe will respond to your intent – in every moment.

In order to be free to contribute and open your field of awareness, your mind and body must be united and you must also be physically, emotionally, and spiritually healthy so that you can be free of stress, tension, anxiety, and the inability to relax. Say Paul Bauer, "At the time a trauma first occurred, a part of our own Self literally became disconnected in order to prevent you from ever feeling that pain ever again. There are parts of you that are much smarter (and faster) than your conscious mind and these parts take on the trauma so you don't have to. Once that part of you takes on the trauma to prevent you from being hurt again, it puts up a wall between you and ANY experience that it thinks is similar. At a very deep level – we are the ones who created our blocks. . . This old conditioning blocks your awareness that you are not separate from what you want. The only separation that exists is within yourself." This blocked condition is the Number One reason that you cannot connect to the Source and transform your life into one of health, wealth, and prosperity.

The highest level of attainment in *qigong* is to get the *shen (*consciousness / mind) into a pure and calm state. When you can breathe deeply and relax, you can connect easily with the Source without distraction. The art and science of Qigong states that your Qi determines the state of your health. If Qi, blood, and oxygen are flowing freely in a balanced manner throughout the body, you have good health. If Qi becomes blocked, stagnant, or imbalanced in some manner, illness or injury will follow. Jindao Health Transforming Qigong detects and resolves energetic imbalances using specific hands-on and hand-off methods and techniques, which include:
• Inducing and balancing energetic pulsing within the body's energetic points, centers, internal organs, joints, cavities, and glands
• Releasing energetic blockages within the body's spiraling pathways
• Controlling the movement of Qi through the body's channels while either projecting or absorbing energy
• Activating dormant energy channels.

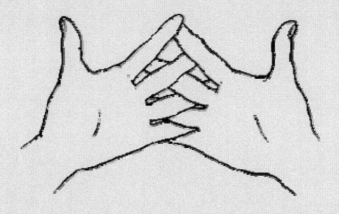

The Treasures that One Seeks in Life Can Only Be Found Within - January 30, 2011

During a Jindao Health Transforming Qigong session (aka: Healing), blocked or stagnant energy (be it physical, emotional, spiritual, or whatever) is released and there is a catharsis that leaves you feeling free and clear of your pains or illness. During a session, rather than focusing on the pain or illness, which gives greater power to it and causes it to grow bigger and stronger, the focus is on growing the remaining wellness until it blossoms forth. When the release occurs, there is often a sudden insight in the true cause of the pain or illness, bringing deeper understanding of what the body was trying to tell you.

In much the same way, when you face problems (situations that cause stress, tension, anxiety, and the inability to relax), if you think and ponder and continue to fight against them, things just get worse as this CONFLICTED state starts to spread out to other aspects of your life. The left side of the brain uses logic to "solve" problems and fights and struggles to force things to come out according to this logic. Being in a fearful state, your left side of the brain wants to be in charge and its insistence on using logic to force a solution becomes the very thing that prevents any solution from coming through. It says that 'you MUST DO something, you need more of this or more of that, you are not trying hard enough, you must measure up, and so on'. In this way, your mind actually creates the STRESS you feel! And, it stifles your creative insight to find a better way (not harder way).

Obviously, logic doesn't work here. In fact, the left side of the brain processes only 7 to 40 bits of information per minute while the right side of the brain processes MILLIONS of bits of information per minute! Logically (ha, ha!), I would trust my right side of my brain to work things out. The right side of the brain uses INSPIRATION, which activates INTUITION, which activates EMOTIONAL GUIDANCE (feelings), which activates INSPIRED ACTION to achieve results.

It is necessary to ask yourself, "Who is doing the driving?". In other words, where are my thoughts coming from that are responding in a negative way (stress, anxiety, tension, etc.)? More often that not these thoughts are HABITUAL unconscious beliefs that have been imposed on you. When problems arise, you have to remove yourself from this state of wanting and lacking and from unconscious beliefs that hold us back from finding a solution. There comes a point that you have to take personal responsibility for your habitual thoughts, your actions, and thus, the RESULTS that are showing in your life.

According to Paul Bauer, author of Effortless Manifesting, your mind has unconscious believes that say that "I'm bad with love, money, health, energy, recognition, self-esteem, confidence, whatever it might be. So if I can step back long enough, and let go of my mind's ability to try and control it all, even if the mind fears letting go, that's okay. And maybe I can have some peace in that moment. I can come back into the presence. I can live in the now for just a moment in time. That's all you've got to do."

Just like physical pain in the body comes from emotional blockages and is trying to get your attention, likewise ("as above, so below; as within, so without") whatever stress you have in your life is literally trying to get your attention. Sometimes screaming for your attention! Says Paul Bauer, ". . . imagine the stress that comes up in your life is like a basketball and you're in the water and you're trying to push it in. You're trying to push that basketball down and you notice it takes a little bit of energy to get that ball under the water. That ball represents the problem or the challenge or the stress that keeps surfacing. So let's say that you push it down with one arm and then another ball comes up, which represents some other major stress in your life. Something about money, something about someone in your family is sick, a task that you've gotta get done or a series of tasks. All of a sudden now it's a multiple set of balls and you're trying to push those down with your arms. Now you've got your legs and all of a sudden you can't control them any longer. So what if you let go?"

In order to let go, you first have to breathe correctly. Stress accumulates more and more in the body and causes you to tighten up and to breathe from the chest instead of the diaphragm. By breathing softly and gently from the diaphragm, your mind can get quieter so that you can calm down and let go. The more you feel that feeling, the more bottled up energy comes up and out your nervous system. Meditational breathing as practiced by Qigong allows you to "understand what the signals that are coming up and out of your nervous system really are, what that energy is, why it's there in your body to begin with and what it's trying to say".

According to Paul Bauer, "The point is to have the intent of having peace with that which doesn't feel peaceful within you. What comes after that, what comes into your life when your mind is calm, when you don't have a polarized mind in other words, one that says I want it. I don't have it. If I could only have it, then things would get good. And that constant feeling of separation. That's what I mean by polarized. It's split into two. I don't have it, if I only could, I'd feel better. And that's the cause of our suffering. . . One of the biggest false premises [based on an unconscious belief] is that we're separate from the very thing we want most. . . Intuitively, you know that you're not separate from anything. You're not separate from your Source, your God, your Creator, whatever you call God in your life. Despite the religious upbringing that you might have gone through, despite the systems that you've been through, whether it be the schools, the familial systems, the media that you watch, they all have done a great job trying to prove that you're separate in some way from who you really are. Until you shift your intent along the way and you find someone, you find a mentor, you find a teacher, you find a friend, you find a book… something that helps you remember something in you and a light turns on. It kind of scares you sometimes at first or it just gives you pause. . . If what you want isn't here right now, it's because your mind thinks that it's not here. And it keeps creating a field where you can't see it, you can't feel it, you can't sense it. It's when the mind lets go and there's a greater force within you that turns things on for you. It's not outside of you, that greater force, it's within you right now."

Continues Paul, "If you feel you are not getting what you want, you might ask yourself, 'How am I giving to others?' If you're not getting what you want the signal you're getting back is the way you've been doing it isn't working for you. So it's just sending you a signal back… okay, this way doesn't work. You might want to consider another way. What could that other way be? Until you let go, you don't know because your way, the way that the mind is thinking it needs to control it, may not be the way. You've got to find what the way is and I don't mean it's outside of you. I mean letting go of the mind. So since creation is always teaching us the simplest way of how to create, all you've got to do is listen. If you're creating what you want with ease, then you are tuned in, you're into it, into your intuition power. Because if you're "off path", that's when you're having stronger difficulties and friction and static and resistance in your life. The more you don't think you have what you want, the more you think that you've got to go out and get it, the more you think that it's not being given to you, etc. It creates that constant cycle of not enough and I have to continue to do something in order to get something. And all that while, it's literally depleting energy from your vital organs, from your brain to your kidneys. The great myth is that we need to attract the stuff we want and "get it" in order for us to feel better."

This means that YOU HAVE EVERYTHING YOU DESIRE ALREADY, but you aren't in the place within yourself yet to see it around you. Your stressing makes you not see it. Ask yourself "What if I could have this in my life right now, how would I feel right now? If this was real in my life right now." Continues Paul Bauer with some VERY important points, "Close your eyes, take a deep breath, and tune into that feeling of what if this was real right now. Continue to breathe all the way to your belly. Feel that feeling. Just continue to breathe into that. Notice that. Notice the shift that just happened within you. That's the beginning of cultivating your sacred self. That's the real you. Ask yourself "How often do I spend time here?" "How often do I allow myself to be in this place, this feeling?" If the answer is not often, that's the reason why you don't have it yet. Because guess what? It is real right now. The only problem is the mind doesn't notice it. The mind can't create it for you. I don't have to attract stuff. The reason why is because I am that which I intend. The moment I intended, it's real. Just like that. Even if my mind can't see it, can't feel it, can't taste or touch or smell it, yet I know it's here right now. It's noticing what's going on inside you, noticing what those thoughts are that are feeling other than peace and tuning into them and shifting the intent from unconsciously saying I don't have it to you know what? Thank you. It's here right now even if my mind doesn't yet see it or feel it, you can breathe into that. . . There's a part of your mind that's called a reticular activating system and it focuses on stuff and it filters stuff out. The reason why you think you don't have what you want is that part of you has been told to keep it out. So the RAS is doing its job. It's doing what it was told to do a long time ago. It's almost like a prime directive. It's protecting you. It's a law within you and it says do not let her or him go there because if they do they're going to get hurt again just like when you were a child. . . It was there the whole time but your mind was filtering it out. . . Whatever it means to you in your life whether it be money or recognition or health or love or radiant energy or confidence, whatever it is. If you don't have it, there's a part of you that's intending for you not to and that's the part of you that you haven't yet made peace with, that you haven't integrated, that you haven't given the love that it wants most. That's what it wants most dearly from you is your love . . . because the thing that I thought I wanted was the thing that I needed to give myself first. Whatever you feel denied of is the thing you deny yourself. Whatever you don't have is something that you're withholding from yourself."

Since we are created from the unconditional giving of The Source, we are made of this creative Source energy. Wanting creates more not having, but whatever you think about most you create in your life. So, letting go and accepting that you already have everything now allows you to tune in to your creation already being real. Connecting to The Source connects us to the power of pure intent. Intent is just pure energy. Intent is pure creation. Your deepest pain has a positive intent for you in some way. Continues Paul, "Maybe I'm going to begin to shift my intent from "this is a bad thing in my life" to "maybe it's got positive intent and maybe it's actually a good thing, but I haven't yet noticed it with my mind". So as I begin to cultivate that peace within me and its positive intent, I notice that this block turns into a "Go" sign, a green light. In fact, it will give me the very energy that I want the most because within the block lies incredible trapped energy and power in such vast amounts that it will blow you away. It will liberate you. It will free you. It will open your mind and it will give you a sense of ease in your body that maybe you've never imagined. So instead of treating it as a block, treat it as a gift. And you listen to its lesson."

Once calmed, you can ask yourself "WHAT is the lesson to be learned from this situation?" Asking open ended questions activates the right side of your brain, which engages the intuitive part of your mind. So, by stopping to ask yourself "what are the lessons that I am supposed to be learning here so I can transcend this situation now" or "what is the positive intent of this challenge", something inside you comes through to bring you insight. This insight brings self transformation as a sudden release occurs that explains what the lesson to be learned is. The "Aha!" moment happens, which brings great calm and clarity, just as "healing" brings cathartic release. Thus, the more you breathe when things are though, the more you can accept, the more peace you bring to yourself, and the more effortless results you will see in your life.

A final word from Paul Bauer: "Close your eyes, take a nice deep breath all the way down to your belly. (breathe in… and breathe out…) And feel your connection to Mother Earth. (breathe in… and breathe out…) And know that you are complete, that you're loved, that you're safe, and that you're whole. You are enough. You are enough. Everything you could possibly imagine is within you. There's no need to go outside of you to have it or to be it or to feel it. It's here right now within you."

Doing Nothing - February 11, 2011

When one desires to meditate, one literally does nothing. First one breathes deep and slow and one either stands, sits, or lies down, with eyes closed. No actions are performed with the body. One becomes conscious of thoughts arising. These thoughts appear suddenly and randomly and are ignored until they slowly cease to occur. Soon enough, one is simply doing nothing other than just being there. A gap of nothingness is observed between thoughts. Within this gap, one observes there is Nothing and that all thoughts arise from this Nothing. During this state of meditation, one observes (becomes conscious of) a natural feeling that arises from this Nothing and develops further in intensity. First one feels stillness, then quiet, then peace, then joy, and then bliss (the sum of the other feelings). This feeling is unconditional; it does not depend on actions or outside events to stimulate it into existence. This unconditional feeling is not like the reactive and conditional feelings of happiness, anger, sadness, guilt, remorse, tread, worry, pride, and so on that must depend on something else (an event, idea, or thought) to stimulate their existence in the mind/body.

This unconditional feeling allows one to realize that there something to observe. When there is something to observe, the Self exists from out of Nothing. Furthermore, this Self exists regardless of any thoughts or reactive feelings. In many traditions, when the self becomes aware of itself, it is called Knowing. One thus becomes aware of that which is unchanging, without beginning nor end, a True Source from which all arises. As consciousness automatically turns inward, the mind/body becomes aware of the Self and also of the Source of the unconditional feeling, which is Nothing. Once Self Aware, one realizes that the Self was always there in the background regardless of ages and events, always observing. One knows that everything comes from one Source, and that there is no movement really and that everything then is an illusion because all comes from Nothing. One knows that there is only now, the past, present, and future existing all at once.

Once one knows that the Self is not separate from this True Source, the Self drops away merging with everything and nothing and one enters the meditative state that is called Pure Awareness. One realizes that there is no movement within the True Source, since it is Nothing, there is only Pure Awareness. Pure Awareness is discussed in many ancient traditions, such as Hinduism, Buddhism, Taoism, and Kabbalism. Everything that exists, every created thing, is the unmoving, non-existent illusion of Pure Awareness. Pure Awareness is everywhere at once and is thus Pure Being. Thus, the Self manifests itself from out of Pure Awareness.

As even Quantum Physics will attest, everything that exists in the universe came from one Source and before that source there was Nothing. Thus, from Nothing came everything. Nothing is not separate from all that is created from it. Thus, Nothing is not empty. It is the point at which all energy stops moving, where all waves cease to vibrate; but it is also a point where all things can potentially arise from and do. Physicists call this Nothing (this Source of all things), the "unlimited field of potentiality". Because everything that exists comes from this Nothing, because the unconditional feeling (mentioned previously) comes from this Nothing, because all thoughts come from this Nothing, because the Self comes from this Nothing, because Pure Awareness comes from this Nothing, one is able to be one with Nothing and Everything at once. Here, all things are possible.

To connect with the place where all things are possible, one simply has to "do" nothing. You already are there since your thoughts, unconditional feeling, and your Self arise from it. Breathing deep and slow is the trigger that puts one into a meditative state where one can observe the gap between thoughts. Here the Self transforms into Pure Awareness and merges with everything and the source from which everything arises, which is Nothing. The Self can let go of wants and needs since they are unnecessary blocks to peace and joy. One can instead state an intention of what one desires (become aware) and Pure Awareness will connect to the Source and all will come to you. Trust the Source to do what is best for the Self. Effort and control are contrary to bliss.

"Embrace the Invisible - Being in the State of Grace" - February 20, 2011

(IMPORTANT NOTE: All the previous postings I have made so far about Qigong all lead and evolve to this particular posting! Re-read them as necessary.)

Qi in Chinese means not only "Breathe / Energy / Life Generating" but also VERY importantly "to issue forth". Gong means "Techniques/Methods/Ways/Skills" literally. Qigong as a term not only means "Breath/Energy/Life Generating Methods", but also "Breath/Energy/Life in Motion". In the science of physics, 'energy in motion' means energy transforming; since the science of Physics has discovered that everything is made of vibrating patterns of energy that come from one issuing forth point that came from Nothing and that this energy is always transforming from one state to another. Also, this Energy ultimately is composed of photons, which is moving Light.

Thus, the whole universe, everything that exists, is made of something that is INVISIBLE. Furthermore, the science of Molecular Biology has discovered that our bodies not only are made of this invisible original source vibrating energy on a molecular level, but also are composed of a rich variety of minerals, 70% water, and mostly empty space, all of which compose a crystalline being. You are an energy "soup" filled with countless energetic frequencies and patterns.

Both sciences have discovered that all molecules are composed of particles within waves of light and that the components of these molecules PULSE in and out of view. So, 50% of the time you exist and 50% of the time you and everything else is again INVISIBLE! Where are you when you are invisible? You and everything that exists returns to the Source, the state of nothingness where all vibrational waves stop moving, where all comes from and all is possible. Thus, you and everything that exists are ONE thing, of ONE source. The pulsing IS life transforming from one state to another, which in Qigong is the life generating concept of 'yin & yang'. Thus, it can be realized that Qigong in general and Jindao Qigong in particular is about Life Transformation because of all these points.

When applying the Qi generating methods, Life Transformation is the end result of a process where the body/mind/spirit is coordinated into one healthy being and inner peace & joy arises as one connects to this Source. The Source is also known as The Tao/Dao (The Way), The Divine, Spirit, God, Goddess, and so on. So far in the previous posts, we have been talking about reaching and staying in this Source. Thus, Jindao Life Transformation Qigong is ultimately about being present in what many and varied spiritual traditions call "A State of Grace" - being under Divine INFLUENCE. This Influence (spiritual self realization) allows us to transcend our base humanity and 'Embrace the Invisible', the Divinity that creates and empowers us. From the Divine Source (and thus you and everything) all that was, is, and could be arises from and gives forth from; from here there is only unconditional giving issuing forth, which is another way of saying "Unconditional love". Also, we have been talking about how you don't have to do anything to receive this unconditional love, you just have to be there and accept it. So, it's not a Doing, it's a Being. You just have to sit still and know (pure awareness), let go, breathe, and be here now.

Meditation, which is quieting the mind to experience peace, is one tool to generate more awareness. Through meditation, you are able to 'stop the world' and connect directly to the Source. At the Source, where there is the pure awareness that experiences the Nothing from which all thoughts emerge, there arises a transformational state of grace where there is first stillness, then quiet, then peace, then joy, then bliss. During this state of grace, you can go even further into ecstasy and beyond even that to where not only your mind/body/spirit unite but you feel at one with Nature, at one with all creation itself. Here, you can not only 'know yourself', but also "know the Divine". When communing with the Divine, you instantly know that all that you that you knew was insignificant, that all the answers you thought you had, all the conclusions to you thought you had, were finite and small next to the vast infinity of the Divine. Here, you realize that you have only questions for the Divine, that the more that you are in its presence, the more questions you have and the more you wish to receive from the Divine.

Many spiritual traditions from India, China, and elsewhere *focus on inquiry as a means of quieting the mind and remaining in the energy of curiosity, rather than conclusion.* If the question is correct, the answer will obviously follow. This idea has been the deepest level of awareness and hidden understanding of Spirituality for thousands of years: from shamanism 5,000 years ago, to Taoism, to Tantra, to Buddhism, to Zen, to Kabbalism, to Judaism, to Christianity, to Hawaiian Kahuna-ism, and forward into modern times with Neville Goddard's Power of Awareness, to Ekhart Tolle's Living in the Now, to Dr. Robert Anthony's Deliberate Creation, to Paul Bauer's Effortless Manifesting. to Kam Yuan's Yuan Method, to Richard Bartlett's Matrix Energetics, to Frank Kinslow's Quantum Entrainment, and so on. The common thread in all true Spiritualities is the concept of "The answer is in the question". Asking questions means being open to all possibilities; open to the giving nature of the Source. Thus, "To Question is to Receive".

Telling the Source your answer blocks your receiving of what could be best for you. Questioning frees you from the bondage of what you think you see before you. Presumed preconceived notions (that is: answers, judgments, and conclusions), stop the flow of energy in your life. More than that, just about all your conclusions were developed under the influence of others (parents, school teachers, peers, friends, enemies, society, nation, culture, and so on) as you were growing up. These conclusions influence your world view, your attitude, your feelings towards yourself and all that you do, your point of view (what you observe on the wave). These conclusions that you draw (from others) create all the limitations in your life. Your point of view creates your reality, rather than your reality creates your point of view. Thus, you can ask yourself, 'What if everything you think and everything you see actually creates everything you see in your experience of your life?' AND NOT THE OTHER WAY AROUND.

Asking the question, allows for there to be something different. Thus, you are living in the question. By 'Being the Question', you allow for possibilities. When you access The Source, by asking questions, it allows for all possibilities to occur because it creates a space for transformation to occur. The question creates more possibilities, while the "answer" (pre-conceived conclusion) limits possibilities. Having a specific point of view creates energetic limitations. If you resist or react, you are creating an energetic limitation. Resistance or reaction connects you to negativity. Allowance is never resisting or reacting against nor aligning or agreeing with. Being open to all possibilities means that The Source can Flow to you and bring you Divine influence. You need to 'Do Nothing' and just accept being in the Flow, you thus 'Choose Change' by being open to receive. In this way, life becomes unhindered, easy, and flowing. Being open to the Flow from The Source brings so much fulfillment that the result is always great joy, and with that there follows gratitude. By choosing change you choose a life of Joy and Gratitude. The questioning allows you to BE the energy for things to change, rather than to be the reaction to things that happen to you. The real truth is "Ask and you shall receive". To make life easy and joyous, you can change present reality by being open to the flow of all possibilities from the Source. To receive, you ask "what would it take to . . ."; "What else is possible?"; "What would it take for this to change?" To create a life transformation, ask "How does it get any better than this?", regardless of when things are "good" or "bad".

The next thing to understand is that your willingness to receive is what opens or closes the receiving. T here is the willingness to actually receive and the clearing of any energy that is in the way of receiving. At this point, you make space for Life Transformation by using tools to clear every past and present thought, feeling, pain, and so on.   Easier said than done? That is because we have lived blinded to what is really there around us, waiting and ready to be accepted. All that we have learned and experienced from childhood when we were ignorant of the Source has influenced us to be wary of pain in whatever form. Thus, we in essence create a gatekeeper between what happens in the outside world and what you allow inside. This gate keeper fears the unknown and clings to the familiar to keep safe. This condition creates instead more pain, stagnation, and blockages and divides us into body/mind/spirit.

According to Dr. Robert Anthony, "The function of the Gatekeeper is very simple. It's basically to keep things the same. Its primary intention is to make your life easier by rejecting information that doesn't match the Subconscious Blueprint you already have inside. In this way, you don't have to keep making new decisions. So the Gatekeeper is designed to keep information out . . . it is useful to stop you from doing stupid things that hurt you . . . it's also very harmful when it keeps you stuck with a belief or habit that you don't want anymore. The Gatekeeper has some very powerful tools at its disposal, which include emotions like fear, doubt, worry and anger. These are psychological defense mechanisms that automatically reject new information. So the key is learning how to instantly bypass your inner gatekeeper and get directly to your subconscious mind -- when you learn to do that, you can change your inner blueprint in moments..." Internal resistance by the Gate Keeper (the Ego) hinders the receiving.

Jindao Life Transforming Qigong uses various methods/ skills/ techniques/ tools to dissolve these blockages and stagnation and to release the pain and fear so that one can Embrace the Invisible. We can live a life either enriched by it all, or in fear of it.

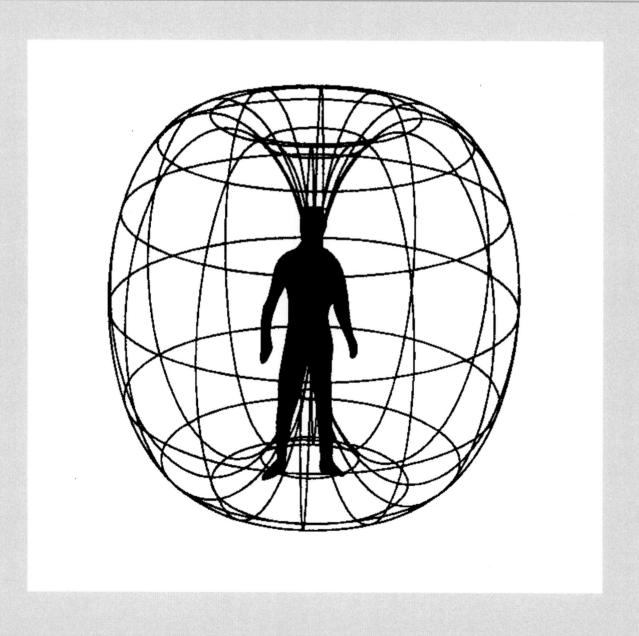

"When a door is always in use, the hinges will never rust" – Chinese saying - March 6, 2011

Qigong is the oldest scientific tradition on earth, and its ideas match quantum physics & molecular biology. The types of Qigong can be divided by its purpose, whether that's creating health, healing others, spiritual development, or martial arts. Qigong uses a very large number of techniques to enhance energy production and flow in your body, including all kinds of massage, breathing methods, movements, and more. First and foremost, Qigong is about increasing awareness and focusing attention to create intention. Taoist Longevity solutions reverse the aging process, boost vitality, and transform the self physically, emotionally, and spiritually.

Through the practice of Qigong techniques, you can master the use of mental attention to connect directly with any part of your body. This focused attention, which is cultivating awareness, unites mind and body and spirit. By observing, you can change your physical properties: electrical activity, electrical resistance, and molecular structure. The positive results increase energy and boost vitality, increase blood circulation, enhance oxygen circulation, and relieve aches and pains. Eventually, you will feel like you can breath into the bones as you focus all your mental attention on the tips of your fingers and continue breathing, feel something like air or energy entering your finger tips as you inhale and exiting your finger tips as you exhale. This feeling spreads through the whole body and eventually you can direct it anywhere you want it to go, both inside and outside your body.

Within a short amount of time and daily effort, Qigong will:

- fix your posture,
- strengthen your muscles, tendons and fasciae,
- take your joints through their total range of motion,
- correct your breathing,
- compress energy into your fasciae, muscles, organs, body cavities and bones,
- renew your blood and oxygenate your cells,
- and give your central nervous system and your energy circulation system a total make-over.

Qigong gives the BENEFITS of jogging while using relaxed stillness within movements:

1) Improves motion of blood circulation and increases levels of neurotransmitters in blood.
2) Stimulates appetite, sexual functions, assimilation of nutrients, aid digestion/elimination.
3) Accelerates metabolism, weight regulation, and sleep regulation.
4) Boosts immunity, and reduces stress induced cortisol.
5) Develops dexterity, reflexes, and prevents osteoporosis; opens joints, stretch muscles, and enhances balance.
6) Allows greater brain-based microcirculation, stimulating bioelectric currents.
7) Enhances mental sharpness, focus, and concentration.
8) Restorative healing, calming effect brings peace of mind – cerebral cortex calms down.
9) Harnesses Universal Source Energy, improves healing, and helps spiritual growth.

Wai Dan Qigong Methods: by focusing on the meridian "water pipes" help keep energy flowing smoothly through the body for health, stress relief, and well-being. They use the limbs to encourage smooth qi flow through the meridians. As qi builds up in the limbs during practice, it will eventually flow back through the meridians to the internal organs to nourish them. Any excess of qi in the meridians will be "siphoned"; off into the vessel "reservoirs"; for storage.

Nai Dan Qigong Methods: by focusing on the vessel "reservoirs" help develop abundant energy for the entire body. They use primarily torso movements, especially in the major joints such as the shoulders or hip sockets, and/or mental concentration to generate and store qi in the reservoirs. As abundant qi becomes available, it will "overflow"; the reservoirs into the meridians, helping to clear out obstructions and smooth out qi flow.

Neigong Methods: to maintain the integrity of your energy, Qigong always emphasizes proper body mechanics. Vitality is lowered by non-articulation of the body; from all of these you get increased vulnerability to disease from a weakened immune system (degenerative diseases and pathogens). Diet & nutrition follows proper body mechanics. Now matter how much healthy food you eat and supplements you take, they are nothing if you do not have a body that works efficiently and effectively.

Often people absorb tension into their bodies and it gets stored in the joints, causing joint pain and inflammation. Also, stress gets stored in the organs causing blockages and illness. Traditional exercises work from the outside in and can overtax the muscles, causing more stress and tension. Working from the inside out instead entails lengthening and strengthening the ligaments and tendons. The job of the ligaments is to connect bone to bone and they provide joint stability. The job of the tendons is to connect bone to muscle and they store and transmit energy.

Often people work out for hours at a time in the gym and get little results to show for it. Now matter how much time or effort they put in, they don't get the results that they are looking for. The bodies still lack tone and they don't feel any stronger. Other people either can't to go to a gym or physically aren't able to exercise because of an injury, aging issues, or illness. Both groups can benefit from learning 'Neigong' inner energy and strength training to develop their bodies from the inside out. Since ancient times, the Chinese Qigong system has contained inner core building methods called Neigong, which literally means "inner work". The simple and easy to learn techniques of Neigong involve standing in place or walking while doing special movements so that the body is aligned and the joints and ligaments are strengthened. The techniques do not require weight lifting or pumping the muscles. Neigong also provides much energy to the body, enhancing one's vitality, rejuvenating and de-aging the body.

According to renowned Qigong master Ken Cohen, "Qigong is one of the most cost-effective self healing methods in the world. The only investment needed is time, a half-hour to an hour each day; the dividends of better health, increased vitality, and peaceful alertness accrue daily and are cumulative."

Transformational Living - March 13, 2011

Energy flows through the body in specific pathways, which Qigong calls Meridians (which means 'channels'). The goal of Qigong is to have a smooth flow through these pathways. If not, blockages are caused which dam up the body, causing a feeling of congestion, tiredness, loss of vitality, aging, and more. Energy blockages are also experienced as pain and disease. Also, through trauma and attitudes, thoughts effect feelings, which in turn negatively effect the physical body. Energy blockages lead to stagnation, which leads to inflammation, which leads to infection, which leads to infestation (parasites). So, a downward spiral from subtle to dense occurs.

Doing energy work (Qigong) is as vital to living healthy as is eating, sleeping, and exercising. Tension, stress, anxiety, and so on accumulate inside us all day, regardless of how calm we are. We cannot attack or escape from the irritations of bosses, bills, or traffic jams; this lack of discharge of pent up stress wears us out over time, leading us to exhaustion or even explosive anger. As people get more tense, they soon get more numb. This accumulation of negativity causes a gradual loss of awareness physically and emotionally. People become less able to know what feeling good actually feels like. They become accustomed to feeling weak, tired, bored, and numb.

Feeling energy is the first step towards taking control of your life. By increasing your awareness of subtle energy, you can start to unravel the layers of negativity. The fundamental movements of basic Qigong help to begin the process of coming back to being fully alive, rather than in a zombie like state. You become aware of not only the physical anatomy (organs, bones, muscles, tendons, ligament, nervous system, lymphatic system, blood vessels, spine, etc), but also the Energetic Anatomy, which consists of its own pathways, vibratory frequencies, and functionality. The Energetic Anatomy can be likened to wireless antennas and how they connect people to the source of a signal and to other people, creating wireless communication. This "wireless communication" allows for transformational living to be possible. Transformational living is the process of generating changes that remove stagnation and that increase the efficiency and effectiveness of your life.

Within Qigong, this process of transformational change is symbolized by the Yin-Yang image, which shows light coming in, shadow going out, and harmonic stillness unifying the two. The Yin-Yang moves the way that energy moves. Energy transforms in three phases: pulsing in, pulsing out, and stillness (rest). All the molecules within our body and within everything in the universe do this alternating between pulsing in and out and resting in between. Within the body, rhythmic pulsations move in a cycle from the extremities to the core. All bodily systems follow this pattern of going in, going out, and stillness, from the blood to the breath to the nerves and so on.

The expansions and contraction that occur during Qigong clear out blockages and stagnation in a way that can be immediately felt. This newly unbridled energy can then be used by you to fight germs, heal injuries, process disturbed emotions, develops creative solutions to problems, and much more. By doing Qigong, you learn to tune in to the innate intelligence possessed within this unblocked energy flow.

Once aware, you can assist it in its natural healing or transformational work. This awareness is what Buddhism calls "mindfulness". You become sensitive to what you feel and thus to who you are. You learn to listen to your self. By being fully able to feel your body's functions, you can more clearly feel your body's boundaries. Then, when you shift your awareness from your body to YOU, you can realize that YOU do not have any boundaries, that you are infinite. Thus, you also learn that your body is within YOU, not the other way around.

Walking Qigong - March 20, 2011

Walking Qigong is a very powerful method of practicing energy movement and healing. Practicing Walking Qigong is very enjoyable thing to learn to practice outdoors in the upcoming spring and summer times. It helps you to lose weight, tone your body, and become more fit and happy; with continued practice you become more relaxed and happy. Not only are the physical, emotional, and spiritual centers opened but coordination and balance are strengthened as well. Immediate movement of Qi is felt through the hands and then rest of the body.

"As the world's fastest race walking gerontologist, I have discovered that blending Qigong movement and exercise has helped me stay healthy and maintain my world class ranking in my age group." - Jack Bray

Medical science has for some time known that the action of walking aids in the return circulation through the venous system. No one had suspected that under the arch of the foot covered by the plantar fascia was a bio-mechanical pump activating an entire system of deep veins responsible for the re-circulation of venous blood to the heart. Walking, not running in a manner that allows the heel to touch down first with the weight of the body rolling over the arch of the foot onto the toes will compress the Plantar heart pump on the feet in the most efficient manner.

The movements protect against osteoporosis, arthritis, weakness, heart disease, and fatigue, bringing you more vitality, rejuvenation, and flexibility. Grounding, proper alignment, posture, weight shifting, breath work, energy movements, self healing, and more are all coordinated together while walking in a special pattern from side to side. Practicing qigong also has positive results on regulating the respiration and oxygen of the body. Medical research has shown that an insufficient supply of oxygen can increase the growth of cancer. When the body is rich in oxygen, the cancer cells die. Walking Qigong allows for greater oxygen content in the body.

Another important factor is the stability of one's emotions. Walking Qigong, while a healing form, is a walking meditation. By obtaining a state of meditation, one is not distracted by depressing thoughts or worries. The feeling of helplessness is lifted and a positive attitude emerges. Through relaxation, the body returns to a more normal state. A feeling of happiness and confidence helps to maintain a strong and vital spirit. This feeling of confidence is also achieved through group practice. One becomes more committed and willpower is strengthened. When the group has good results, all are encouraged and keep a positive outlook, which aids in the healing process.

In the beginning, Walking Qigong involves stepping and landing gently with the heel first, rocking forward and pushing off from the toes—heel, toe, rolling, when the leg goes forward, bend the knee. This works better than stepping forward with a flat foot or over striding. There is also a method where you walk with a series of steps in snake-like moves to the left and then to the right like weaving in and out, as if your path would resemble the winding progress of a snake. There are many different walking patterns with many different arm postures. Most people are conditioned to focus on walking in a straight line forward; this pattern gives the brain a chance to work on left/right integration as you move forward. The movements first to the left and then the right will harmonize the two sides of the brain as well as help the mind and body become one. With each step, you breathe deeply in a natural way, while the arms can be down at your side or up in various Qi gathering and moving postures.

"Be aware of the contact between your feet and the Earth. Walk as if you are kissing the Earth with your feet. Each step we take will create a cool breeze, refreshing our body and mind. Every step makes a flower bloom under our feet. We can do it only if we do not think of the future or the past, if we know that life can only be found in the present moment." —*Peace is Every Step: the Path of Mindfulness in Everyday Life* by Thich Nhat Hanh

Wu Wei - Doing Without Doing - April 3, 2011

At the very heart of Qigong training, coming from its Taoist roots, is the idea of "Wu Wei", which is Chinese for "Effortlessness". It also means "doing without being fake". Wu Wei is an important concept that involves *knowing when to act and when not to act*. Wu Wei has also been translated as "creative quietude," or the art of letting-be. Wu Wei is about letting the Tao or Source of All flow through you so that your life is not a hard struggle; it is about not straining or forcing things to happen but letting them happen as they should in due time. For example, Trees grow by growing, not be "doing something" to grow. Planets revolve by revolving, not by "doing something" to revolve. Thus knowing when (and how) to act is not knowledge in the sense that one would think "*now*" is the right time to do "*this*", but rather just doing it, doing the natural thing. Qigong, in the form of Neigong, is also used to even make the practice of martial arts become effortless. It is used so that you can adjust your balance, body alignments, posture, and movements so that you can move and be with Effortless Power. The aim of *wu wei* is to achieve a state of perfect equilibrium, or alignment with the Tao or Source of All, and, as a result, obtain an irresistible form of "soft and invisible" power.

Being in a state of Wu Wei means knowing the power of letting go. The distinguishing characteristic of Taoism is that of being natural. According to meditation master Bruce K. Frantzis, "*Wu wei* is not "non-action", but action that operates by simply following the natural course of universal energy as it manifests without strain or ego involvement. Ultimately, *wu wei* boils down to recognizing what exists at the absolute depth of your heart and mind. Rather than allowing your ego to get involved, you find relaxation and letting go of any need to *do*. When the ego is active, strain and stress follow." Qigong and especially Qigong Meditation methods teach you to use their full effort without strain. If you can remove the strain, then any action becomes relatively effortless by definition. Continues, Bruce K. Frantzis, "In this light, "not doing" doesn't mean you don't do anything. You can raise your hand, which is an action, but it's a fairly effortless action if you're a healthy human being. Ask yourself these questions: Can you remain relaxed enough that you don't tense, force, apply your mental will or project your energy outward to accomplish a task? Can you allow action to naturally and spontaneously emerge from within you?"

In the beginning, one encounters Internal Resistance. Just ask yourself, for example, something like, "What if I didn't have to work?" and then see how suddenly the chatter inside the mind comes up and starts giving you a million reasons why you have to "work". This resistance is the Ego looking to preserve the status quo to keep you safe, to prevent any unknown and unforeseen consequences. But, any time you are uncomfortable you are growing. Letting go of this internal resistance is letting fear go. Fear is taking a past experience and projecting it onto a future experience, which totally destroys the moment where an opportunity can be received. Fear starts in the past and future and denies the present. But, by letting go of what no longer serves you, you can take action and take the steps that will prevent your future from becoming your past! Hanging on to feelings (resentment, anger, hurt, shame, etc.) or judgments or conclusions force you to be in your own way, these emotions block you, stagnate you, and congest you. From there physical injury starts to develop in the body, in the form of pain, inflammation, infection, and infestation. So, there is a big relief in letting go. Qigong allows you to observe what you have blocking you inside, breathing through it, and letting the sigh of relief release the stagnant emotion. You feel the block opening and this trapped energy moves out and goes higher and higher from where it was locked in until it is no longer felt inside again.

Taoist Qigong meditation teaches you how to put forth as much effort as possible without strain. We start by defining the line of effort and strain with simple qigong exercises. Says Bruce K. Franztis, "Through practice, you discover that if you cross the line— if you go past a certain point in body or mind—an internal fight arises, you hit internal resistance. The trick is to figure out how far you can go forward without encountering resistance of any kind. When you play the line without overdoing it, you can achieve more and progress faster. However, as soon as you strain, internal resistance begins to build. Keep in mind that this line of effort and strain is constantly changing. Where you find yourself today is not necessarily where you will be tomorrow or six months from now. So it's not as simple as identifying the line once and staying behind it. Taoist philosophy recognizes that the Universe already works harmoniously according to its own ways; as a person exerts their will against or upon the world they disrupt the harmony that already exists. This is not to say that a person should not exert agency and will. Rather, it is *how* one acts in relation to the natural processes already extant. The *how*, the Tao of intention and motivation, *that* is key." So, Wu Wei is letting go and then taking action in a way that feels natural, like it was always meant to be.

According to Wikiipedia, "It is not an imaginary state that we aspire to but one readily achievable and frequently entered by those performing repetitive movements which require energy and concentration. It may be experienced by athletes, performers, musicians, ramblers, students of the nei jia (the internal schools of martial arts) students of the wai jia (the external schools), yoga practitioners, students of certain schools of meditation and others. The majority of those who have entered wu wei have no fore-knowledge of the event and only know that something extraordinary happened that they couldn't put into words. . . The goal for wu wei is to get out of your own way, so to speak. This is like when you are playing an instrument and if you start thinking about playing the instrument, then you will get in your own way and interfere with your own playing. It is aimless action, because if there was a goal that you need to aim at and hit, then you will develop anxiety about this goal."

One of the biggest problems or obstacles that people put in their own way is being impatient; of not allowing themselves time to integrate what they have learned through Qigong or elsewhere within themselves. Continues Bruce K. Frantzis, "Over the years, I've observed many students try to go around the line. The ones that are successful at advancing their qigong, bagua or tai chi practice (and life in general), know that when they hit any internal resistance, they've just got to switch to something else for a while. They take a rest and allow time for integration. Once whatever is causing the resistance is integrated, they can once again move forward. If you can observe yourself and see how much you can do while remaining relaxed and open, you might find that you can't do as much at first. Back off—whether in your practice or your daily life—and maintain a level of output that doesn't cause tension. Then, as you begin to do more, tasks will become easier without the necessity of activating your force of will or the drama that has become common to the modern man. In modern life, we're constantly chasing after things in the external world. But you will never find peace in any external object. Any external object you get will eventually become boring and lose its appeal. Practicing the principle of *wu wei*, of effortlessness, will allow you time for integration. In the internal arts, you learn form in order to master a technique, then you forget the form, and eventually experience the formlessness of *wu wei*. This formlessness is the ultimate goal of all the internal arts. This fundamental Taoist concept of action arising from an empty mind without preconception or agenda will help you discover the joy and happiness inside yourself."

Eating Air - April 24, 2011

The ancient Taoists regarded deep breathing as a form of nourishment. During deep breathing, you not only fill the body with purifying oxygen, but also guide universal energy (Pre-Natal Qi or Chi) in and out of the body as well. This nourishes the Post-Natal Qi that you were born with but deplete as you age, greatly rejuvenating your body. The fact is, the full amount of oxygen that the body requires is MORE than what regular everyday breathing can provide. The deep breathing that results from strenuous activity is required by the body, as our ancient ancestors did while hunting and farming, in order to force you to inhale more air.

According to Qigong master Bruce Frantzis, "Unfortunately, most people have poor breathing habits. They take shallow breaths, only use a portion of their lungs, even when they believe they are taking deep breaths, and hold their breath--especially when they become nervous or tense. . . Breathing with the whole body has been used for millennia to enhance the ability to dissolve and release energy blockages in the mind/body, enhancing well-being and spiritual awareness. . . Studying your breathing patterns can make you aware of the ways your moods and emotions change. For example, fear tends to produce erratic, strained or weak breathing patterns. Holding the breath is often a preceded by violent, angry explosions. Likewise, holding the breath without realizing it is part of a reaction to stress and tends to increase its severity. Shallow breathing makes people prone to lung weaknesses in the face of environmental problems, such as polluted air, and can also lead to depression."

While hard physical activity can be exhausting, the act of deep breathing itself is not. The practice of Qigong (breathing or energy movements) brings large amounts of oxygen into the body with barely any energy cost to it. In fact, slow deep breathing burns fat, which gives us much more energy than the burning of carbohydrates do when performing physical exercises like body building and aerobics in the gym. The saying is "Where intention goes, Qi follows. Where Qi goes, the blood follows". Fully oxygenated and energized (Qi filled) blood kills organisms that cause disease, eliminates infections, and clears meridian blockages, altogether resulting in healing!

Qigong deep breathing techniques, says Bruce, "get everything inside your body moving and in synch with the rhythm of your breathing. It wakes up the inside of your body and makes it incredibly healthy. The methodology cultivates your ability to relax at any time and concentrate for long periods. . . (It):

- Facilitates oxygen intake and the balances the oxygen-carbon dioxide exchange in the body
- Fully expels carbon dioxide
- Retrains your nervous system to relax
- Improves the functioning of your internal organs
- Increases Qi reserves in the body. "

According to Yan Gaofei, "Chinese Medicine teaches that tension (stress) will block the continuous smooth flow of chi. Because chi is the "leader" of the blood, poor chi circulation will negatively influence the blood circulation causing the body to grow improperly. Without the nourishment provided by a strong chi/blood movement, our body becomes "dry" and stiff, unable to optimize organic performance. Good chi and blood flow enable the body's systems to be "fluid" and soft in order to be successfully functional. Without good chi/blood circulation the total body, its organs, and its systems (nervous, circulatory, digestive, etc.), falls out of natural harmony resulting in sickness, weakness, systemic breakdowns, stress related illnesses and disorders. Chi flow stimulates blood flow and together they are vital for a good interchange of the internal energy necessary for good health. When you develop the ability to relax completely and go into a deep "quiet," in time, you will reduce and eventually reverse the damage produced by pressure and emotional or physical strain. Initially it may appear that nothing has changed outwardly but, in fact, much has changed internally."

The Jindao Life Transforming program's natural energetic transformational exercises are based on ancient Qigong and Neigong movements that help balance the body from the inside out, producing three major changes in the body:

1. Helps to rid the body of stagnant energy that is not moving freely. Stagnant energy is located where there are physical, emotional, mental, and psychic blockages.

2. Raises the body's energy levels so that its own natural healing capacities are stimulated and become strongly elevated.

3. Helps to balance the body's energy flow through the meridians and deeper energy channels and vessels.

The famous Dr. Oz, Oprah's medical guru, on his television program, also espoused Qigong as a way to "add years to your life", to reduce stress, promote longevity, cardiovascular care, and help alleviate chronic pain and fatigue symptoms. Qigong makes your body pulse with energy. Only Qigong deals with the actual energy itself to such a degree that it causes our body to regenerate.

Thus, the practice of "eating air", which is Qigong, greatly revitalizes the body in every way. After learning the proper breathing methods and physical movements, Qigong practice on a much deeper level includes visualization, intent, and deep concentration with subtle changes in energy development. Cultivating relaxation and looseness through both meditation and physical activity helps Qi flow through the body with unimpeded circulation, channeling Qi where it is most necessary. Qigong allows you to manipulate Qi for many purposes, including: pain relief and self healing, organ and neuro-lymphatic health, self-defense, and psychic and personal development.

Regardless, since it is a form of nourishment, Qigong is something that must be practiced regularly, with the commitment to incorporate it long term in one's lifestyle. Without this commitment, Qigong's amazing benefits are temporary. With everyday practice (even for 15 minutes a day), Qigong brings long years of healthy physical, emotional, and spiritual purifying, healing, and nourishment.

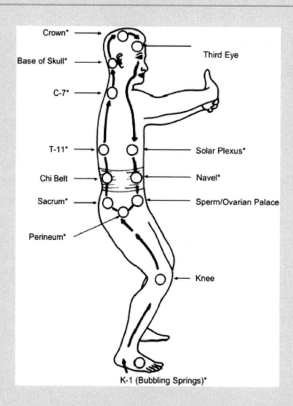

Emotional Healing - Do You Live Life or Does Life Live You? - May 22, 2011

Life's up and downs can often trigger emotional responses, which are either healthily expressed or unhealthily repressed inside. The Emotions (which can be seen as "Energy" in "Motion") are a powerful part of our being. Emotions of any kind cause strong feelings in the body and in the mind. When the body and the mind are not in harmony, it makes us feel confused, unhappy, and ill at ease, hence, dis-ease begins. Just imagining happy or sad feelings or thinking of a happy or sad situation will cause you to feel positive or negative emotions. According to Traditional Chinese Medicine dis-ease is caused by emotional repression. People think that strong emotions are "bad" and they avoid feeling them. Trauma, resentment, grief, or grudges can become locked in the body's tissues and organs. Such repressed emotions get held in the organs of the body and each emotion is associated with a particular organ. The liver stores anger, the kidneys hold fear, the spleen holds worry, the lungs hold grief and sadness, and in the heart repressed emotions can cause depression and a lack of joy. Repressed emotions can slow down circulation to the organ and toxins can build up.

For example, lung and respiratory problems may result when sadness is repressed. Blockages in the kidneys may lead to reproductive, bone, ear, and other problems when fear is repressed. Anger issues such as resentment can cause problems with the Liver. In her article, " Moving into Thankfulness with Qi Gong " (published in the *New Health Digest* , November 2003), Lisa B. O'Shea states "Resentments can be big or small and can cause huge stress on our physical and emotional well-being. Chinese Medicine and Qi Gong look at this resentment as relating to the Liver energy system. The Liver system includes the liver and gall bladder, their respective meridians, the eyes, glands, tendons and ligaments, the peripheral nervous system, as well as nonphysical elements such as decision-making, action taking, and the emotions of anger and frustration. Symptoms such as depression, anxiety, cancer, ovarian cysts, fibroid tumors, endometriosis, constipation, headaches, allergies, twitches, muscle cramping, PMS, or menopausal problems can all come from the stress on the Liver energy from bottled up emotional resentment."

Stress, anxiety, tension, and the inability to relax also affect us by building up static electricity in the body. This static causes blockages, which cause stagnation, which causes congestion, which causes inflammation, which causes infection, which causes infestation. The calmest person in the world is still subject to outside factors that wear away at one's wellbeing. It has recently been proven by scientists that the body cells hold memory; thus, emotions repeatedly felt set up a pattern of vibration within the cellular memory of a given organ. These emotions adversely affect decision making and action taking. The good news is that Qigong, and Jindao Life Transforming Qigong in particular, offers great relief from emotional effects. The various self healing movements practiced in Qigong help to restore balance to the body, mind and emotions, not by reviewing the emotional issues, but by releasing the trapped emotions from the organs and body tissues. The Four Core Points of Qigong (Posture and movement; Deep Breathing; Massage; and Meditation) all work together to unwind the body, release the trapped emotions, and harmoniously unify the body, heart, and mind. Upon this release, we begin to feel unification, peace of mind, and self transformation.

How does Qigong do this? Qigong movements exchange energy (Qi) between people and the universe. The greater concentration of energy (Qi) from the Universe flows into areas that are deficient in Qi and restores them back to harmonious levels. This can take minutes, hours, days, or weeks, depending on the severity of one's condition. Once the emotions are balanced, the body calms itself. According to Qigong master Li Junfeng, "Qigong is good for overall health. Through the exchange of qi, diseased qi is removed and fresh qi is gathered. Qigong brings about the removal of negativities that lead to worry, sadness, anger, nervousness, fear, and a stressful life. As a result, one is free to lead a happy and carefree life. Modern medicine is good but only provides a temporary solution. If people want to maintain their health the energy level in the body must be in balance - the emotions must become balanced and even. Emotions can affect the physical body. The emotions and the physical body must be in harmony. This determines the quality of life. Finally, qigong opens the heart. As one experiences the opening of the heart, this allows the qi from the universe to go to the entire body, removing the negativities that rob one of a life of perfect well-being."

The ancient Chinese Qigong masters taught the importance of connecting spirit to body or the Heavens to the Earth through ourselves. In essence, we become an antenna between the cosmos and the Earth. In Jindao Life Transforming Qigong, one is taught how to receive and transmit unconditional love through exercising intention. Continues Li Junfeng, "The true qigong awakens understanding from the heart so people can have a natural life rooted in unconditional love. Qi is never separated from love. Through the practice of qigong, true love is always with you - the joy of the lightness of being is always with you. A healthy mind coming from the practice of qigong cooperates with the flow of qi in the body. In the end, one realizes that it is not that the heart and the mind are used to make the qi flow effectively. It just happens naturally, of its own accord. Then life is never seen apart from the qigong state. It is then that one's life becomes established in it."

When we encounter emotional upsets, this is exactly the time when you should practice Qigong! Using your brain-mind to solve your problems is to no avail. No matter how many times you ask, your mind has no clue on how to solve your problems. If it did, you wouldn't have any! Instead, your heart-mind (xin) is the place to direct your attention. Receiving and transmitting Qi to the heart field here harmonizes the internal flow of energy and disperses the stagnant energy trapped inside. In this way, you can move your low energetic vibrations to a higher vibratory state of Joy and Gratitude arises as we see how things truly are and appreciate what we have. Instead of dwelling on what is wrong, we start from a point of wellness and blossom out from there. Upon release, the result is always a big smile and a sudden laugh as the nervous system balances out as well. Daily Qigong practice makes it easier and easier to laugh at the daily aggravations and frustrations that happen. Thus, 'you live life', instead of 'life living you'!

ROOTING - The Foundational Support of Qigong - May 29, 2011

The Goal in the art and science of Qigong is to BE Balanced as Efficiently and Effectively as possible. The Result is that your internal energy ("Jin" in Chinese) has Effortless Power. In the study and practice of cultivating Qi and effortless internal power, one of the most important principles is the concept of rooting. Rooting is having perfect balance so that you can move efficiently and effectively, without disjointedness and without struggle. Rooting is one of the means that Qigong uses to transform your life from dis-ease into one of Joy and Gratitude.

You develop root by studying what the body must do in order to keep the weight's center balanced while moving slowly, eventually adding more and more speed. People lose root because they use the wrong part of the body to focus their strength. For example, when the shoulder moves first in an action, it is incorrect. One should use the lower body to drive the force. No matter how hard one attempts to be soft, they will never truly relax and have effortless power until the lower body drives the force.

In the article, *"Rooting, the Secret of Getting Power from the Earth"* by Gaofei Yan and James Cravens, explains what rooting is: "Rooting is the process of making a good connection to the ground in stances and during transitions. ... When we refer to rooting, we are talking about rooting the legs (and thus the entire body) of the completed postures, as well as the legs during the transitions as well. When we are trying to achieve rooting in Taijiquan [Qigong], we should visualize below the surface of the floor or ground... much like the roots of a tree. The "Bubbling Well" an acupoint called Yong Quan (KI-1) located on the bottom of the foot should be used as the point from which this imaginary root extends into the ground from which to draw strength. Rooting in Taijiquan [Qigong] will transfer from foot to foot, but never stays equally rooted on the right and the left. The weight should remain on the outer edges of the feet and remain a slight gripping feel with the toes, the ball of the foot, and the heel. Although the Yong Quan never touches the floor, you should still focus on this area as the root of each movement."

Yan explains how rooting effects your Qigong practice: "when one uses the lower body to drive the force, the root can be lost because the shoulder, as well as any other joint or part of the body may interrupt the transference of power. When there is tightness or loss of coordination between the various joints and parts of the body, root will be lost. The hip, leg, etc. must act as one! Many times things inside the body fight against each other. For example, if the inguinal crease (part where the legs connect to the torso) at the hips is tight, the flow of energy will be broken in the body, breaking the root. When one practices in this way, the tightness or lack of body unity can give one the tendency to get injured. Sometimes one locks a joint. The hips and shoulders are typical joints that students will lock which breaks the root. At the other extreme, the body can be too loose or limp which will also cause the root to be broken.

Other causes that disrupt a continuous root include psychological reasons. Being frightened suddenly is a common example of how one's energy will rise, taking away the potential power from the ground through rooting. Other emotions, such as anger, happiness, sadness, and being excited, can all play a role in losing root since they distract the mind from its focus. Finally, the reason for a lost root is often a combination of several postural problems. When one loses root, his movement or force cannot change directions and his body is segmented and not unitary. Internal power should be round and unitary, not linear and segmented. Roundness has the quality of continuation and flow, while linear does not contain this quality and will cause the body to stop and start, producing a segmented non-unitary action."

When having root, the body moves as a whole unit. Continues Yan, "when one loses root, several factors are involved: the amount of tension in the muscles, the way in which the body connects and works together, and the ability to produce a powerful product in terms of projection. . . In order to have a proper root, movement should never go by arm alone but by the whole body. The weight is transferred by turning the body. . . Without lower body emphasis, there is no rooting. . . In Tai Ji Quan [and Qigong] one moves very slowly, balancing over the Yong Quan points in the bottom of both feet in order to find and control the center of the weight. This assures that the force can come from the ground and not be stopped inside the body. Furthermore, the front leg must also screw [in to the ground] and not be "loose" so that the whole body can contribute to power going out of the hand. The sensation is that the ground below moves in opposite directions due to this inward screwing with both legs. A loose front leg creates a large energy loss going out the front knee. In Tai ji we say that the front leg has no 'Peng Jing' [warding off energy]." Further, says Yan, "In order to have root, certain things must be true about the body, the movement, the Qi (energy), and the mind:

Body

1. The body should be straight. The body sinks and the head hangs as if suspended or pulled upward lightly from a string. This opposite stretch creates a straighter spine which then allows muscles to relax, giving more flexibility and movement to the body.

2. The waist must sink; sometimes one side may sink. This sinking has always been recognized as necessary in rooting.

3. Muscles on both sides at the inguinal crease should relax. If one does not relax, chi will not go down into the legs. This also aids in the process of straightening the lumbar curve in the back.

4. Two Huan Tiao (the points just behind the side hip bones) must be rolled back and out; these are also acupuncture points.

5. The distance between the upper inner thighs (dang) is the same width at the front of the inner thighs as at the back of the inner thighs. For example, if one assumes a toe-in hour glass stance, the distance at the rear of the inner thigh is greater than at the front. If one tucks the hip forward, the distance at the front of the inner thighs is greater than at the rear of the inner thighs. In Yang style Tai Ji they say they put the whole body on two legs, and the Chen style of Tai Ji explains this by saying it is like taking a seat or a sitting position while standing. The upper inner thighs should have a shape like an upside down letter "U" and not like an upside down letter "V."

6. The acupuncture point called the Huiyin or perineum, as well as the anus, is internally pulled upward. This keeps the small heavenly circulation or the chi unblocked.

7. The "Wei Lu" refers to keeping the lower back straight during the posture or movement.

8. The entire body through to the legs must screw inward which will open the inner thighs. The knee should not be inward, but should be lined up straight with the foot's direction so that the power from the ground will not be broken. One will actually feel an outer pressure on the outside knee as the legs screw inward toward the ground.

9. The acupuncture point "Wei Zhong," located on the leg behind the center of the knee should always be strong. The knee will have to be bent and not kinked inward in order for this to be right.

10. Toes should grip the ground and the Yong Quan points (located just below the ball of the foot but just on the toe half of the foot) in the bottom of the feet become empty, which contributes to all movement and stability. The Yong Quan points are also known as the "bubbling well."

Qi (energy)

The Qi in the body will flow properly when the three acupuncture points are lined up properly. These points are:

1. Bai Hui - located on the crown point.

2. Hui Yin - located between the genitals and the anus; this point should close and lift.

3. The intersection between the two Yong Quan points. The intersection is somewhere between the feet depending on the posture.

These three points should all be lined up vertically. One cannot overemphasize the need to relax. When the three points are lined up in a relaxed manner, the Zhong Qi (centered Qi) gets larger. Qi is a difficult subject for those just beginning to study, and the concept of centered Qi is difficult as well.

Mind

The mind and spirit must be strong in order to keep Qi from rising, which will destroy the effort of rooting. The mind must be very centered and controlled. Many people practice Chan (Zen) exercises, or something similar, in order to accomplish this. This, of course, has a parallel in life since the mind must also be kept centered every day in order to handle all circumstances.

When practicing, one should use imagination so that one can image clouds or a river to create evenly flowing movement. One can go fast yet stay quiet. When traveling in an airplane, one feels very still even though the speed may be 500 m.p.h.. Enemies to the mind are anger, fear, and various other emotions and distractions. They raise the chi high in the body, making the body tight and again destroying the root.

All of these requirements to building root support each other and connect to each other in a complimentary fashion. After a long time you will understand the beautiful harmony of the requirements. The straight plumb line requirement causes the thigh to go in, but when one takes the two points in the hip out the knees move out opening the thighs up properly. Another example of harmony between the requirements is that when the legs are down and when one sinks, the practitioner can use the whole body as a unit."

Qigong (and Tai Ji Quan) sets up the root initially by standing in the Wu Ji posture. Wu Ji refers to absence of movement. From the Wu Ji comes the Tai Ji ('from nothingness comes everything'). In the Wu Ji posture, you can feel the three points in one line in order to feel the centered Qi. The weight should be centered over the yong quan points in the bottom of the foot. Rooting makes you feel centered, which has a calming effect as the Qi sinks down into the lower body. You feel like a Big Tree, part of nature, timeless and endless. This harmonious state allows your movements and perceptions to join and follow (give and receive) with your inner self, other people, and the environment you operate in. Finally, since Yan, "The Tao Teh Ching was written by Lao Tzu who described the way of the universe. This book told people how to control the world. Its conclusion was that you control the world by controlling yourself - that you have more control in this world if you simply learn to control your own self and balance." Rooting allows you to be fully aware of what things feel like in such a complete way that you are in direct communication with the reality of the moment. It puts you in the driver's seat.

How does Qigong HEAL?

By raising energy high enough to push through blockages in the circulatory and nervous systems (like blowing through a straw to clear the path). A blockage is a small area where blood cannot fully go or where disease can occur. Qigong improves blood flow and opens blockages by relaxing the body so that your INTENTION can guide the blood through to closed off capillaries. Studies show that Qigong activates 90 percent of the brain.

Qigong increases the level of circulation to the body, organs, glands, and nerves, which rejuvenates the body, mind, and spirit. Increases Longevity and reverses aging process; results in significant memory improvement, learning, and enhancement of the physiological functions controlled by the brain. Mediation is done with breath work and movements to help relax the body further to promote healing, such as:

Moving Meditation – heals while also making richer, thicker brain pathways and connects to the Insula, soothing the limbic Brain, relieving stress.

"Mindful Meditation" - body is totally relaxed while moving in a meditative state.

Qigong gives the BENEFITS of jogging (without the stress and boredom) while using relaxed stillness within movements:

1) Improves motion of blood circulation and increases levels of neurotransmitters in blood.

2) Stimulates appetite, sexual functions, assimilation of nutrients, aid digestion/elimination.

3) Accelerates metabolism, weight regulation, and sleep regulation.

4) Boosts immunity, and reduces stress induced cortisol.

5) Develops dexterity, reflexes, and prevents osteoporosis; opens joints, stretch muscles, and enhances balance.

6) Allows greater brain-based microcirculation, stimulating bioelectric currents.

7) Enhances mental sharpness, focus, and concentration.

8) Restorative healing, calming effect brings peace of mind – cerebral cortex calms down.

9) Harnesses Universal Source Energy, improves healing, and helps spiritual growth.

Health practitioners NEED Qigong as they can became drained, absorb aches and pains of their clients, and may use incorrect body alignment and improper posture.

Practice in groups amplifies energy greatly. Biological magnetic field of each person joins to create a large group field. High amplitude energy heals people in a powerful way.

1 person = 5 units of energy. Person doing Qigong alone = 25 units; w/ 3 people = 150 units; w/ 10 people = 700 units; 500 people = 100,000 units.

"Emotional fitness": Qigong > Awareness > Attention. Meditational Qigong = Paying attention to HOW YOU THINK. Thoughts, Energy, and Intention work together. You choose your emotions. On a basic level, your own patterns of THINKING and FEELING lead to the ACTIONS you take and the BEHAVIOR you display. Qigong helps in GETTING PAST FEAR and "CONNECTING" ON A DEEP LEVEL. Negative feelings, more often than not, lead to NEGATIVE EMOTIONAL EXPERIENCES. If you are in CONTROL of your EMOTIONAL EXPERIENCES and have a handle on your own emotional state, then you can consistently create more POSITIVE EMOTIONAL EXPERIENCES.

Matter = knots of Energy. Energy is made of light. Light comes from Universe. Universe is created of thought. Universe = Giving Energy; Earth = Receiving Energy; People = Sharing Energy – the intersection between "heaven and earth".

TRUE SHARING > Resistance against ego > Reveals the Light by Sharing.

"I receive not for myself alone but in order to share."

"You have to Give in order to Get". Giving is receiving.

"It's not what you want, but what you got"

Five Stages of Qigong Development: 1) Mind-Body Awareness; 2) Coordination of Breath with Mind-Body; 3) Rooting & Energetics; 4) Silk reeling – Waist rotation and alignment; 5) Spiral energy body.

Emotional Healing - Do You Live Life or Does Life Live You?

Life's up and downs can often trigger emotional responses, which are either healthily expressed or unhealthily repressed inside. The Emotions (which can be seen as "Energy" in "Motion") are a powerful part of our being. Emotions of any kind cause strong feelings in the body and in the mind. When the body and the mind are not in harmony, it makes us feel confused, unhappy, and ill at ease, hence, dis-ease begins. Just imagining happy or sad feelings or thinking of a happy or sad situation will cause you to feel positive or negative emotions. According to Traditional Chinese Medicine dis-ease is caused by emotional repression. People think that strong emotions are "bad" and they avoid feeling them. Trauma, resentment, grief, or grudges can become locked in the body's tissues and organs. Such repressed emotions get held in the organs of the body and each emotion is associated with a particular organ. The liver stores anger, the kidneys hold fear, the spleen holds worry, the lungs hold grief and sadness, and in the heart repressed emotions can cause depression and a lack of joy. Repressed emotions can slow down circulation to the organ and toxins can build up.

For example, lung and respiratory problems may result when sadness is repressed. Blockages in the kidneys may lead to reproductive, bone, ear, and other problems when fear is repressed. Anger issues such as resentment can cause problems with the Liver. In her article, "*Moving into Thankfulness with Qi Gong*" (published in the *New Health Digest*, November 2003), Lisa B. O'Shea states "Resentments can be big or small and can cause huge stress on our physical and emotional well-being. Chinese Medicine and Qi Gong look at this resentment as relating to the Liver energy system. The Liver system includes the liver and gall bladder, their respective meridians, the eyes, glands, tendons and ligaments, the peripheral nervous system, as well as nonphysical elements such as decision-making, action taking, and the emotions of anger and frustration. Symptoms such as depression, anxiety, cancer, ovarian cysts, fibroid tumors, endometriosis, constipation, headaches, allergies, twitches, muscle cramping, PMS, or menopausal problems can all come from the stress on the Liver energy from bottled up emotional resentment."

Stress, anxiety, tension, and the inability to relax also affect us by building up static electricity in the body. This static causes blockages, which cause stagnation, which causes congestion, which causes inflammation, which causes infection, which causes infestation. The calmest person in the world is still subject to outside factors that wear away at one's wellbeing. It has recently been proven by scientists that the body cells hold memory; thus, emotions repeatedly felt set up a pattern of vibration within the cellular memory of a given organ. These emotions adversely affect decision making and action taking. The good news is that Qigong, and Jindao Life Transforming Qigong in particular, offers great relief from emotional effects. The various self healing movements practiced in Qigong help to restore balance to the body, mind and emotions, not by reviewing the emotional issues, but by releasing the trapped emotions from the organs and body tissues. The Four Core Points of Qigong (Posture and movement; Deep Breathing; Massage; and Meditation) all work together to unwind the body, release the trapped emotions, and harmoniously unify the body, heart, and mind. Upon this release, we begin to feel unification, peace of mind, and self transformation.

How does Qigong do this? Qigong movements exchange energy (Qi) between people and the universe. The greater concentration of energy (Qi) from the Universe flows into areas that are deficient in Qi and restores them back to harmonious levels. This can take minutes, hours, days, or weeks, depending on the severity of one's condition. Once the emotions are balanced, the body calms itself. According to Qigong master Li Junfeng, "Qigong is good for overall health. Through the exchange of qi, diseased qi is removed and fresh qi is gathered. Qigong brings about the removal of negativities that lead to worry, sadness, anger, nervousness, fear, and a stressful life. As a result, one is free to lead a happy and carefree life. Modern medicine is good but only provides a temporary solution. If people want to maintain their health the energy level in the body must be in balance - the emotions must become balanced and even. Emotions can affect the physical body. The emotions and the physical body must be in harmony. This determines the quality of life. Finally, qigong opens the heart.

As one experiences the opening of the heart, this allows the qi from the universe to go to the entire body, removing the negativities that rob one of a life of perfect well-being."

The ancient Chinese Qigong masters taught the importance of connecting spirit to body or the Heavens to the Earth through ourselves. In essence, we become an antenna between the cosmos and the Earth. In Jindao Life Transforming Qigong, one is taught how to receive and transmit unconditional love through exercising intention. Continues Li Junfeng, "The true qigong awakens understanding from the heart so people can have a natural life rooted in unconditional love. Qi is never separated from love. Through the practice of qigong, true love is always with you - the joy of the lightness of being is always with you. A healthy mind coming from the practice of qigong cooperates with the flow of qi in the body. In the end, one realizes that it is not that the heart and the mind are used to make the qi flow effectively. It just happens naturally, of its own accord. Then life is never seen apart from the qigong state. It is then that one's life becomes established in it."

When we encounter emotional upsets, this is exactly the time when you should practice Qigong! Using your brain-mind to solve your problems is to no avail. No matter how many times you ask, your mind has no clue on how to solve your problems. If it did, you wouldn't have any! Instead, your heart-mind (xin) is the place to direct your attention. Receiving and transmitting Qi to the heart field here harmonizes the internal flow of energy and disperses the stagnant energy trapped inside. In this way, you can move your low energetic vibrations to a higher vibratory state of Joy and Gratitude arises as we see how things truly are and appreciate what we have. Instead of dwelling on what is wrong, we start from a point of wellness and blossom out from there. Upon release, the result is always a big smile and a sudden laugh as the nervous system balances out as well. Daily Qigong practice makes it easier and easier to laugh at the daily aggravations and frustrations that happen. Thus, 'you live life', instead of 'life living you'!

Chinese Characters for Qi Gong:

What is Energized Food-Based Healing?

Food-based healing is the practice of using specific foods to reverse specific diseases. There have been millions worldwide that have reversed type 1 & 2 diabetes, cancer, heart disease, asthma, and even have had dramatic improvement for children with Autism – with food alone.

Naturopathic medicine has tested the effectiveness of such natural remedies. You can learn about blending fruits and vegetables into "smoothies." For example, things like, the avocado's "big" seed is tasteless in a smoothie and has the energy of an entire tree and unique phytochemicals that cleanse plaque from the arteries.

More than the foods themselves, food-based healing is about using special parts of the food where healing compounds are most concentrated. This knowledge is openly shared during my lessons and workshops.

Energized Food Healing

Food is a major factor in health and healing. To live well, one has to eat energized food; eating correctly is another form of Qigong. In order to naturally heal the body, the Jindao System not only teaches what to eat and why, but also when and how often.

Also, taking into account the quality of the food taken into the body is dramatically important. "Garbage in, garbage out" is an important axiom to remember.

Eating for health includes eating organically grown whole foods and drinking organic green juices. Eating raw foods besides cooked is also beneficial.

Eating the right foods not only helps prevent infections, but can also help fight them. Readily available foods (which are inexpensive compared to drugs and surgery) have the power to activate our body's immune system so that it can naturally heal itself. Without proper nutrition the body is too weak to work efficiently and effectively.

Most human illnesses and diseases are due to a deficiency of vital nutrients. When you supply your body with the proper nutrients, in a form that your body can use, it knows how to repair itself.

Organic Foods

Organic fruits and vegetables (and organically fed animals for meat) are free of all pesticides and chemicals, which weaken our immune systems drastically.

In order to relieve inflammation in our body, treat gastro-intestinal illnesses, heal chronic illnesses, and aid against immune system suppression, it is important to only eat organic foods.

The natural energy in our body is negatively affected by eating foods that are not organic because they overload our defense systems and have a toxic effect on our organs, as well as parts of our body.

Whole Foods

Whole foods are those that nature provides, with all their edible parts. Whole foods of vegetable origin include fresh vegetables and fruits; whole grains (millet, brown rice, oats, rye, whole wheat, buckwheat, quinoa, cornmeal); beans and legumes (lentils, chick peas, kidney beans, etc); nuts and seeds.

Fragmented foods include all foods that are missing original parts: refined complex carbohydrates such as white flour and white rice (missing fiber and nutrients found in bran and germ); conversely, the bran and germ of grains (missing carbohydrates); sweeteners (crystallized sugars, syrups, concentrates -- all missing water, some missing most nutrients); refined and deodorized oils and fats (missing both their trace elements and the rest of the plant or animal).

Fragmented foods that have generally been considered healthful include juices and tofu (all missing fiber), bran, wheat germ (missing starch), and vitamin supplements (missing macro nutrients and whatever micro nutrients they do not contain).

One of the major benefits of eating whole grains is that they slow down the digestive process, thereby allowing better absorption of the nutrients. Their fiber content also regulates blood sugar by slowing down the conversion of starches into glucose. Whole grains make favorable changes in the intestines, allowing healthful bacteria to keep disease-producing bacteria in check; they have strong anti-oxidant properties to help protect the body against free radicals, as well as phyto-estrogens and phytochemicals that break down carcinogenic substances.

To insure our nutritional health we need to consume daily one or two servings of whole grains, a serving of beans and/or animal protein, plenty of raw and cooked vegetables of many different colors, and fruit and nuts as snacks.

Phytochemicals

Organically grown whole raw fruits and vegetables contain important life sustaining microscopic healing substances known as phytonutrients (such as Flavonoids), which act as KEYS on our cellular receptors. Phytochemicals are found mostly in the skin, stems, & seeds.

Some are structurally similar to Insulin and fill the cells "insulin keyhole" allowing glucose to enter the cells. Other Phytochemicals in the stem of pineapple help activate PHASE-2 ENZYME, which is the primary detoxification process of the human body undertaken by the Liver. It is this phase-2 enzyme that people need to ACTIVATE for a reversal of cancer. There are over 385 phytochemicals in just one apple.

In order to get these essential phytochemicals into our bodies, it is important to drink juices made from grinding the whole raw fruit and vegetable, using special machines made just for this purpose. These special juicers are not like the typical juicers that remove all of the fiber; instead these machines use all of the vegetable or fruit, even the seeds pits. Sometimes it is not possible to eat raw whole foods (for example, because of digestion or malabsorption problems), so it is very important to drink juices made in this way.

Fresh, raw foods contain the highest level of enzymes, which are the catalyst for the hundreds of thousands of chemical reactions that occur throughout the body. Cooked foods and dry convenient diets have been denatured and are devoid of enzymes- life-promoting elements.

Healing with Food

The fastest way to restore wellness is to stop putting into the body the things that have caused the physical problem to develop in the first place and then give the body the nutrients it needs to repair and rebuild itself. The body is self-healing when the infraction is stopped and proper nutrients provided.

It takes more than just vitamins, minerals, and fiber to be able to label a food a "healing" food. Good foods also contain an abundance of all manner of phytonutrients. These substances are believed to be so powerful that some scientists calling them ""the vitamins of tomorrow". The discovery of phytonutrients has changed everything we know about foods - one of the most exiting discovery is that some foods can literally stop chemical changes that can lead to cancer.

A number of plant foods, such as apples, tea, onions contain substances called flavonoids that can prevent germs from taking hold. One of the most powerful flavonoids is a compound called quercetin. Found in large amounts in onions and kale, quercetin has been shown to damage genetic material inside viruses, preventing them from multiplying. Having several servings a day of flavonoid-rich foods will help keep germs in check, giving your immune system a fighting chance.

"Man's body is a living organism, made of living cells, which require living food in order to be properly nourished and function well. When we put cooked food into our body, loaded with contaminants, the body starts to break down. It begins in the very young with colic, rashes, colds, earaches, upset stomachs, swollen glands and tonsils. As the child grows older, their may be tooth decay, pimples, the need for eye glasses, etc. Then as we enter adult life there is arthritis, hypoglycemia, heart attacks, strokes, diabetes and cancers. All this and a multitude of other diseases are unnecessary and are nothing but the result of improper diet and lifestyle! Today, most people accept cooked food as the normal means of supplying the body with nutrients, not realizing that the living cells of our bodies do not take nourishment from the dead and artificial ingredients found in cooked food. And so, after a typical meal of cooked meat, cooked potatoes, a cooked vegetable and a piece of cooked bread, followed by a cooked sugar desert, their stomach is full and they think they have satisfied the nutritional needs of their body. In reality, they have given their body practically no nourishment. And thus with a full stomach, they are slowly starving their body's cells." From the book, Raw Foods, by George H. Malkmus

The following website provides information on which specific foods help against various ailments: http://www.healingfoodreference.com/

Internal Exercises: Neigong, Weigong, & Qigong Practice

The Jindao System's 'Natural Energetic Healing' exercises are known as "Internal" because they contain Neigong (內 功) - 'internal exercises' and Qigong (氣 功) - 'breathing or energy exercises' methodology at their foundation.

Dao Yin - Chinese Yoga

For many thousands of years, esoteric Chinese Taoists developed physical exercises, breathing methods, and meditation methods that worked the inside of the body to increase one's physical health and spiritual well being; these were called "Dao Yin", which literally means "guiding and stretching". Dao Yin is also known as "Chinese Yoga", since it similarly used to balance, strengthen, and heal the body through physical stretching and standing postures and guided meditation.

Traditionally and historically speaking, Daoyin practices are stretching exercises, usually combined with breath work. This breath work was called "Qigong" (i.e., 'Breathing / Energy Skills'). In this way, work was done inside the body to enhance heal, wellbeing, and longevity. The Eight Section Brocade is one of the most well known Dao Yin methods.

Chinese Yoga has three primary goals:

1. To increase the vital energy moving into and circulating within our bodies.

2. To become aware of the subtleties of our body, breath and mind and understand their relationship to one another, as well as how to use this relationship to create a sense of wholeness and peace in our everyday life.

3. To increase our physical flexibility and strength through full ranges of motion, as well as gain smoothness and depth in breathing. This helps to enhance every aspect of our physical, mental and spiritual wellbeing.

Neigong - Internal Exercises

This "internal" work was called "Neigong". Neigong emphasized coordinating specific body movements with breathing techniques, in specific ways to develop internal strength by 'harmonizing inner and outer energy'. Internal strength was designed to amplify the effect of physical actions while reducing the effort involved in doing them.

Emphasis was placed on the elasticity of the body, the mobility of the joints, the support of the skeletal structure, the twisting and stretching of the organs and connective tissue, and the proper alignment of the body's parts in order to move as a unified whole.

Qigong and Neigong originated through the Chinese philosophy of Taoism (Daoism) with its first recorded history in the *Yi Jing / I Ching* (Book of Changes). Qigong has subsequently been influenced by Buddhist, Confucian and medical beliefs. Currently, it is part of Traditional Chinese Medicine (TCM), along with acupuncture and herbal remedies. Its basic premise is to treat the origin of disease in the whole person – body, mind/emotions, spirit – by looking at the imbalance of the entire human system.

Qigong does this through a system [also used in acupuncture] of both pathways that circulate energy, known as meridians, and of vessels that store energy. Qigong exercises are designed to clear blocked energy in different body organs. It is acupuncture without needles, exercises you can do yourself that induce self-healing.

Some of the basic principles of Neigong are:

• the traditional Chinese belief that the body has something that might be described as an "energy field" generated and maintained by the natural respiration of the body, known as "qi";

• the belief that this 'qi' (i.e., the life energy inside a person) flows and moves though the body and is assisted by the internal organs;

• the release of external and internal tension is a necessity for cultivating health;

• the letting go of muscular strength to perform specific techniques and postures;

• a heightened self awareness of internal body structure and posture;

• the development of 'root' by lowering the body's center of gravity, whereby the origin of movement is lowered within the body, which is believed to cause a sinking of 'qi' or internal energy;

• the combining of the normally separated areas of the body into one integrated, unified, and powerful whole;

• the coordination of specific breathing methods with bodily movements, and the development of an internal peace or calm emotional state;

• the methods involve using the minimum amount of force to achieve maximum results via leverage.

Neigong practices cause the whole body to move in a continuously stretching, expanding and contracting, opening and closing motion. Eventually the body is fluid enough to move very quickly as needed with an absence of central nervous system reaction lag time; great power can be issued with little movement.

This twisting of the body causes the organs to twist as well, which activates the organs to have a detoxification reaction, whereby the liver, intestines, and other organs release toxins that were stored deep in the body so that they can be flushed out. The ultimate aim of this neigong practice was to make the practitioner one with nature, physically, emotionally, and spiritually.

The various Chinese Buddhist and Taoist based martial arts systems that were developed at Wudang, Emei, Kunlun, Shaolin, and other places throughout China at different times incorporated these Neigong techniques and further developed them for use in both health cultivation and "soft" self defense into what today is called the "Neijia" or "internal" family of martial arts. In his book, *The Principles of Effortless Power,* Peter Ralston explains that, "An internal system . . . concentrates on fundamental, natural principles that are mostly overlooked in other pursuits. For example, an internal system has inherent in it relaxing the whole body, using the whole body all at once, deriving power from the ground, intrinsic strength, the use of Qi or energy circulation throughout the body and that cultivation; breathing, the psychology of the whole matter, perceptive skills, developing the area below the navel".

The Thirteen Core Concepts

At the heart of all qigong / neigong methods, and the "internal" martial arts that incorporate them, is an intrinsic set of thirteen core concepts. The purpose of these concepts is to teach one to have effortless power through the most efficient and effective mental attitudes and body mechanics. On one level, they involve mental processes and on another level they involve physical activities. In his book, *The Principles of Effortless Power* , Peter Ralston does a great job of explaining these 13 ideas that are contained within all internal martial arts as "5 Principles and 8 Points" for making the body move more efficiently and effectively:

The *Five Principles* for being effortlessly effective:

1. *Being Calm* – staying undisturbed in the face of adversity; controlling the thoughts, emotions, and energy of the body so that it is empty and calm. In this way, one can deal with the reality of what is happening rather than reacting to circumstances based on preconceived ideas and habits.

2. *Relaxing* – keeping the mind and the body supple, loose, and open. In this way, the body sets itself naturally using its own connective tissues to bind together was a whole, without locking and tightening any of its parts, such as the joints, tendons, muscles, and so on. Energy is able to flow freely and circulate through the body without impedance. Movements can change freely and spontaneously as necessary.

3. *Centering* – putting physical and mental attention into the center region of the lower abdomen (called the 'Dantein') so that it governs all body movement. In this way, the body moves as whole, outwardly from this center point; the center directs the movements that the body follows. A centered body becomes more functional and effective because it has structural alignment and balance.

4. *Grounding* – sinking the body weight (after calming the mind and relaxing and centering the whole body) so that it is carried by the pelvis and legs, lowered into the feet, and finally sunk into the earth. To accept the weight properly, the body weight is shifted to only one leg at a time ('single weighted'), gaining leverage. The body weight is not evenly distributed over both legs at one time ('double weighted'), which could allow one to easily topple over. During stepping, the weight is relaxed from one foot and then transferred to the other foot, hugging into the earth. In this way, energy is moved down so that the body is rooted and support by the ground.

5. *Being Whole and Total* – the entire body works as one unit, with no gaps within body movements. The limbs do not move independently of the center, they move without tension as a result of the center's movements. In this way, the body and the mind's intention move harmoniously from the center in a complete three dimensional manner.

The *Eight Points* on structuring body alignment efficiently:

1. *Align with gravity* – align the structure of the relaxed body so that energy is directed downward. In this way, only a minimum amount of energy is used to hold up the body. The body is balanced so that each part below directly supports the parts above it. We align with this falling energy, which is being pulled by gravity.

2. *Align the Knee, Heel, and Toe* – Movement of the knee is directed down the leg and pressing into the heel of the foot. The front of the knee point in alignment with the toes of the foot, not going past them in any direction. As the foot turns in or out, so too does the direction of the knee. Also, the pelvis stays in between the feet. In this way, maximum leverage is achieved.

3. *Shifting the Weight* – One leg is relaxed before it moves towards the other and compresses into the heel. With one foot free, the steps or the waist and legs can be adjusted without some preliminary movement. The center of the body presses into the foot, which presses itself away from the earth. In this way, the weight is shifted as if dropping into the ground and the body is compressed or squeezed, moving as if it is coming up from the ground (getting great power from the compression). The stepping is coordinated with the breathing, which is sunk into lower abdomen immediately before the foot is pressed.

4. *Unlocking the Body* – the joints of the body are allowed to bend and rotate with ease so that they can relax and align themselves to the way they naturally function. The feet are relaxed so that they act as a suction cup that spreads on the surface they are on and become sensitive to balance; the pelvis is relaxed so the hip joints open so that it drops down and stays between the two feet; the upper body is relaxed so that the shoulder joints open and loosen, keeping the shoulders and elbows pointing downwards; and the joints are relaxed and opened so that the body's balance is maintained and it is not effected by occurring forces.

5. *Integrate, Unify, and Coordinate All Body Parts* – When the various parts of the body move tightly without whole body harmony, the body loses power, balance, coordination, and more. When the major sections of the body move with unification and coordination, it is called the 'Six Unifications" or 'Six Harmonies' (六合 - 'Liuhe'). The lower and center parts take priority over and initiate movement of the upper parts. The moving center allows the foot to move out in relationship with the hand, the hips to turn with the shoulder, and the elbows and knees to move together. The nose always points in the same direction with the naval. In this way, the head turns at the same time as the pelvis. The pelvis is kept directly under the upper body and over the feet so that it is centered between the upper and lower body. Finally, the mind, energy, and body moves as one unit, with energy circulating through the body, permeating all its parts, and then becoming heard and understood so that it can be transcended.

6. *Functional Priorities* – the upper body is subservient to the lower body and the inner center directs the outer body parts. The center then has the highest priority since it creates all movement. Likewise, energy has priority over physical movement.

7. *Creating the Opening for Intrinsic Strength* – making all the relaxed body connections and alignments allow its intrinsic strength to be used naturally and expressed with effortless power. Movement is propelled loosely from the center so that the limbs are emptily projected outwards with a minimum amount of force. As the hands go up, strength is then concentrated away from the arms down into the legs and feet, which then can freely project a maximum amount of power back up through the relaxed arms. Being that the joints are open and the body tissues are loosened, the limbs can elongate greatly and the extending energy can strike from a greater distance than is expected.

8. *Being Three-Dimensional in Eight Directions* – the movement of energy from the center radiates freely and equally in all directions (i.e., front, rear, left, right, up, down, inside, and outside).

Self Defense through 13 Healing Postural Movements

Eventually self defense oriented footwork and hand movements developed over time that exemplified these 13 core concepts. These associated movements often were called the "Shi San Shi" (十三式), which can mean "13 Forces" or "13 Skills" (十三功). Some called them the "13 Powers" or "13 Postures" (十三勢), as well as 13 Tactics, Entrances, Movements, or Energies. The 13 Shi are not actually 13 different and distinct postures, it really means 13 basic skills or attributes for advance study. These 13 Shi were further developed under different names depending on where and when the material was being taught: the 8 Directions and 5 Steps; the 8 Powers and 5 Elements; the 8 Gates and 5 Directions; and so on.

The 13 Shi allowed one to master using effortless power for self defense. The key to achieving this effortless power was to first master rooting through single weighted postures. Once single weighted rooting was mastered, then what was next mastered was rooted movement while the body is relaxed. To achieve this mastery, the body is kept fully relaxed and tension-less by dropping the shoulders and elbows, relaxing the lower trunk, and letting everything be naturally pulled downward by gravity so that all the body's weight is felt in the feet. It was essential to be able to retain one's root while stepping forward and backward; in other words, to walk and shift positions while remaining weighted, or rooted.

To defeat any attackers with effortless power one must bring them out of their range of balance. By evading their attack, they must to over extend to continue to issue force. Next, at the moment of contact, either on defense or offense, the body's weight must be rooted straight into the ground. The body exhales while the supporting foot is being driven into the ground, allowing the weight to fully drop down into that foot. Thus, the body can then achieve maximum leverage to uproot an attacker by unifying the body's weight into a single space under this foot. When the weight is dropped through the feet into the ground, our body is more stable than any moving human force that seeks to come into contact with our body, which allows the body to act as a lever to uproot an attacker.

During stepping, it is important that the point on the foot where the most weight is pushing into the floor is centralized. Once you over extend and use brute force you come out of this strong root, and your power decreases congruently. Also, it is important to understand that by relaxing, staying calm, and "not trying", you can master self defense and uproot an opponent with effortless power. If the opponent enters your space, no matter what technique he is executing, he will be uprooted and toppled easily. The less brute force you use, the more you instead can discharge your *mind/intention* (Yi) to move others. The weight can then be dropped at will while in any posture or movement.

The next step of great importance is learning to turn at your central axis or waistline. When attacked, you can simply turn your Axis and uproot them with little to no force when rooted. When the force is initiated in our direction we relax patiently and begin turning our *axis/waist* slightly to redirect or deflect their energy. The hands guard the centerline while simultaneously acting in defense and offense.

Furthermore, internal Chinese martial arts feature such concepts as:

- Maximum power is used with a minimum of effort because the muscles, ligament, tendons, and will are focused to exercise in coordination with each other;

- "Stopping the Fight", preventing or evading an incoming attack rather than engaging in sports-like one on one trading of blows;

- Evasive maneuvers are used to get out of the way, much like a bull fighter moves out of the way of a charging bull with horns;

- Every technique is simultaneously both offensive and defensive (there is no direct hard blocking first and then a counterattack);

- No first initiation of movement, the attacker initiates, but the defender's movements quickly hit the attacker before his attack can be completed;

- Striking with punches and kicks is deemphasized, instead the emphasis is on taking down an opponent by using the legs, arms, or even the whole body to evade, trap, unbalance, or trip an attacker;

- Often the foot is used during self defense to step on an opponent's foot to help unbalance the attacker;

- All movements are based on pointing, swinging, or both together.

Today, the martial arts of Bagua Zhang, Taiji Quan, and Xing/Xin Yi Quan are the best known of the Neijia arts and are often practiced together. The origins of these so-called "Big Three Internal Martial Arts" are both mysterious and controversial. These convoluted origins are often interconnected and interrelated and span through many other Chinese martial arts. Often times some aspects of one style's boxing routines served as a root to the development of another style, though their relationship may have become long forgotten today.

During the Qing Dynasty (1644 to 1912), many famous Chinese martial artists arose who practiced not only all three arts of Bagua, Taiji, and Xingyi, but also some form of Long Fist Boxing as well, such as Shaolin Quan and Tongbei Quan. One such practitioner, Sun Lu Tang (孫祿堂 , 1861-1932), noticed that there were many similarities between the movements, body mechanics, and core ideas of the boxing routines of the three internal arts and was able to develop a practice that successfully integrated their movements. Sun Lu Tang was renowned as a master of the Chinese Neijia (internal) martial arts and was best known for developing the Sun style Tai Chi Chuan, which contains elements of Chen Bagua Zhang, Hao (Wu) Taiji Quan, and Hebei Xing Yi Quan.

Sun Lu Tang

After mastering Xingyi Quan and Bagua Zhang in Hebei, Sun Lu Tang next studied Yi Jing theory and Emei qigong in the Sichuan Mountains and Taoism, qigong, and martial arts in the Wudang Mountains. In his writings, Sun Lutang said that internal martial arts shared the following characteristics:

1. The use of a relaxed body to coordinate leverage as opposed to the use of brute strength.

2. The development, circulation, and expression of qi within the body.

3. The application of Daoyin, Qigong, and Neigong principles of bodily movement.

Jindao Life Transforming Qigong Theory

by Salvatore Canzonieri

The Jindao System converges various theories that address the nature of humanity and its relationship to the universe, in order to provide 'Natural Energetic Healing' for the body, mind, and spirit.

The most important ideas, among others, in the Jindao System are: "It's not what you want, but what you got"; "You have to give in order to get"; "The Universe is Giving / Loving Energy, the Earth is Receiving / Accepting Energy, and Humanity is the Sharing/ Union of both", which arise from the very ancient philosophies of Taoism, Chan (Zen) Buddhism, Christian Mysticism, Kabbalism, and Tantra.

Taoism

The word *Tao* (or *Dao* , depending on the romanization scheme), literally translates as "path" or "way" (of life) and can figuratively mean "essential nature", "destiny", "principle", or "true path".

Taoist propriety and ethics emphasize the Three Jewels of the Tao : compassion, moderation, and humility, while Taoist thought generally focuses on nature; the relationship between humanity and the cosmos; health and longevity; 'Wu Wei' (action through inaction), which is thought to produce harmony with the universe; emptiness (refinement), detachment , flexibility, receptiveness, spontaneity, the relativism of human ways of life, ways of speaking and guiding behavior.

Tao can be roughly stated to be the *flow of the universe*, or the force behind the natural order, equating it with the influence that keeps the universe balanced and ordered. The flow of Qi , as the essential energy of action and existence, is often compared to the universal order of Tao.

Tao is also associated with the complex concept of *De* - "power; virtue; integrity", that is, the active expression of Tao.

Wu wei is a central concept in Taoism. The literal meaning of *wu wei* is "without action". It is often expressed by the paradox *wei wu wei,* meaning "action without action" or "effortless doing". The practice and efficacy of wu wei are fundamental in Taoist thought. The goal of wu wei is alignment with Tao, revealing the soft and invisible power within all things. It is believed by Taoists that masters of wu wei can observe and follow this invisible potential, the innate in-action of the Way.

In ancient Taoist texts, wu wei is associated with water through its yielding nature. Water is soft and weak, but it can move earth and carve stone. Taoist philosophy proposes that the universe works harmoniously according to its own ways. When someone exerts his will against the world, he disrupts that harmony. Taoism does not identify man's will as the root problem. Rather, it asserts that man must place his will in harmony with the natural universe.

P'u represents this passive state of receptiveness. *P'u* is a symbol for a state of pure potential and perception without prejudice. In this state, Taoists believe everything is seen as it is, without preconceptions or illusion.

P'u is usually seen as keeping oneself in the primordial state of *tao*. It is believed to be the true nature of the mind, unburdened by knowledge or experiences. In the state of *p'u* , there is no right or wrong, beautiful or ugly. There is only pure experience, or awareness, free from learned labels and definitions. It is this state of being that is the goal of following *wu wei*.

Taoists believe that man is a microcosm for the universe. The body ties directly into the Chinese five elements. The five organs correlate with the five elements, the five directions and the seasons. Akin to the Hermetic maxim of " as above, so below ", Taoism posits that man may gain knowledge of the universe by understanding himself.

In Taoism, various rituals, exercises, and substances are said to positively affect one's physical and mental health. They are also intended to align oneself spiritually with cosmic forces, or enable ecstatic spiritual journeys. Internal alchemy and various spiritual practices are used by some Taoists to improve health and extend life, theoretically even to the point of physical immortality.

The Three Jewels, or Three Treasures, (san-bao) are basic virtues in Taoism. The Three Jewels are compassion, moderation, and humility. They are also translated as kindness, simplicity (or the absence of excess), and modesty.

Chan (also known as 'Zen') Buddhism was particularly modified by Taoism, integrating distrust of scripture, text and even language, as well as the Taoist views of embracing "this life", dedicated practice and the "every-moment".

Chan or Zen Buddhism

Chan is a school of Mahayana Buddhism, translated as Zen in Japanese. Chen is in turn derived from the Sanskrit *dhyana*, which means "meditation ". Chan or Zen emphasizes experiential prajña, particularly as realized in the form of meditation, in the attainment of enlightenment. As such, it de-emphasizes theoretical knowledge in favor of direct, experiential realization through meditation and dharma practice. The establishment of Chan / Zen is traditionally credited to be in China, the Shaolin Temple, by the South Indian Pallava prince-turned-monk Bodhidharma, who came to China to teach a "special transmission outside scriptures", which "did not stand upon words".

Through Chan / Zen there developed a way that concentrated on direct experience rather than on rational creeds or revealed scriptures. Wisdom was passed, not through words, but through a lineage of one-to-one direct transmission of thought from teacher to student.

Some scholars also argue that Chán has roots in yogic practices, specifically *kammatthana* , the consideration of objects, and *kasina* , total fixation of the mind. Many historians proposed that Chán was probably an indigenous Chinese creation by mixing Buddhist doctrine with Daoist and Neo Daoist ideas. Some Chinese scholars, such as Ma Tian Xiang even propose that Zen's foundation is based on Lao Zhuang Daoist philosophy instead of Indian Buddhism.

Zen asserts, as do other schools in Mahayana Buddhism, that all sentient beings have Buddha-nature , the universal nature of inherent wisdom (Sanskrit *prajna*) and virtue, and emphasizes that Buddha-nature is nothing other than the nature of the mind itself. The aim of Zen practice is to discover this Buddha-nature within each person, through meditation and mindfulness of daily experiences. Zen practitioners believe that this provides new perspectives and insights on existence, which ultimately lead to enlightenment.

Unlike other Buddhist sects, Zen de-emphasizes reliance on religious texts and verbal discourse on metaphysical questions. Zen holds that these things lead the practitioner to seek external answers, rather than searching within themselves for the direct intuitive apperception of Buddha-nature. This search within goes under various terms such as "introspection," "a backward step," "turning-about," or "turning the eye inward."

Zen Buddhists may practice koan inquiry during sitting meditation (zazen), walking meditation, and throughout all the activities of daily life. Koans often appear to be paradoxical or linguistically meaningless dialogues or questions. But to Zen Buddhists the koan is "the place and the time and the event where truth reveals itself". Answering a koan requires a student to let go of conceptual thinking and of the logical way we order the world, so that like creativity in art, the appropriate insight and response arises naturally and spontaneously in the mind.

There are other techniques common in the Zen tradition which seem unconventional and whose purpose is said to be to shock a student in order to help him or her let go of habitual activities of the mind. Some of these are common today, while others are found mostly in anecdotes. These include the loud belly shout known as *katsu*. It is common in many Zen traditions today for Zen teachers to have a stick with them during formal ceremonies which is a symbol of authority and which can be also used to strike on the table during a talk.

Thomas Merton (1915–1968) the Trappist monk and priest was internationally recognized as having one of those rare Western minds that was entirely at home in Asian experience. Like his friend, the late D.T. Suzuki, Merton believed that there must be a little of Chan / Zen in all authentic creative and spiritual experience. The dialogue between Merton and Suzuki explores the many congruencies of Christian mysticism and Chan / Zen.

Christian Mysticism

Christian mysticism is the pursuit of communion with, identity with, or conscious awareness of God through direct experience, intuition, instinct or insight. Christian mysticism usually centers on a practice or practices intended to nurture those experiences or awareness, such as deep prayer (i.e. meditation, contemplation) involving the person of Jesus Christ and the Holy Ghost. This approach and lifestyle is distinguished from other forms of Christian practice by its aim of achieving unity with the divine.

Whereas Christian doctrine generally maintains that God dwells in all people and that they can experience God directly through belief in Jesus, Christian mysticism aspires to apprehend spiritual truths inaccessible through intellectual means, typically by learning how to think like Christ. William Inge divides this *scala perfectionis* into three stages: the "purgative" or ascetic stage, the "illuminative" or contemplative stage, and the "unitive" stage, in which God may be beheld "face to face".

Within the broad spectrum of religious groups, it is believed that the spirit of man lost its original connection with God. The spirit of man longs to find this connection again and to intimately experience God. Although orthodox Christianity teaches that this connection can only be restored via the blood of Jesus Christ through His sacrificial death, mysticism teaches alternative or supplementary spiritual practices as a way to restore the relationship between God and man. These practices include meditation, purification, and works of love.

For Christians the major emphasis of mysticism concerns a spiritual transformation of the egoic self, the following of a path designed to produce more fully realized human persons, "created in the Image and Likeness of God" and as such, living in harmonious communion with God, the Church, the rest of humanity, and all creation, including oneself.

Christian mystics have pursued a threefold path in their pursuit of holiness. While the three aspects have different names in the different Christian traditions, they can be characterized as *purgative, illuminative, and unitive,* corresponding to body, mind, and spirit.

The first, the way of purification, is where aspiring Christian mystics start. This aspect focuses on discipline, particularly in terms of the human body; thus, it emphasizes prayer at certain times, either alone or with others, and in certain postures, often standing or kneeling. It also emphasizes the other disciplines of fasting and alms-giving, the latter including those activities called "the works of mercy," both spiritual and corporal, such as feeding the hungry and sheltering the homeless. Purification, which grounds Christian spirituality in general, is primarily focused on efforts to, in the words of St. Paul, "put to death the deeds of the flesh by the Holy Spirit" (Romans 8:13). The "deeds of the flesh" here include not only external behavior, but also those habits, attitudes, compulsions, addictions, etc. (sometimes called *egoic passions*) which oppose themselves to true being and living as a Christian not only exteriorly, but interiorly as well.

The second phase, the path of illumination, has to do with the activity of the Holy Spirit enlightening the mind, giving insights into truths not only explicit in scripture and the rest of the Christian tradition, but also those implicit in nature, not in the scientific sense, but rather in terms of an illumination of the "depth" aspects of reality and natural happenings, such that the working of God is perceived in all that one experiences.

The third phase, usually called contemplation in the Western tradition, refers to the experience of oneself as in some way united with God. The experience of union varies, but it is first and foremost always associated with a reuniting with Divine *love,* the underlying theme being that God, the perfect goodness, is known or experienced at least as much by the heart as by the intellect since, in the words 1 John 4:16: "God is love, and he who abides in love abides in God and God in him." Some approaches to classical mysticism would consider the first two phases as preparatory to the third, explicitly mystical experience, but others state that these three phases overlap and intertwine.

Purgation and illumination are followed by a fourth stage which Underhill, borrowing the language of St. John of the Cross, calls the dark night of the soul. This stage, experienced by the few, is one of final and complete purification and is marked by confusion, helplessness, stagnation of the will, and a sense of the withdrawal of God's presence. It is the period of final "unselfing" and the surrender to the hidden purposes of the divine will. Her fifth and final stage is union with the object of love, the one Reality, God. Here the self has been permanently established on a transcendental level and liberated for a new purpose.

Kabbalism - Jewish Mysticism

Kabbalah (Hebrew: lit. "Receiving") is a discipline and school of thought concerned with the mystical aspect of Judaism. It is a set of esoteric teachings meant to explain the relationship between an eternal/mysterious Creator and the mortal/finite universe (His creation).

Kabbalah seeks to define the nature of the universe and the human being, the nature and purpose of existence, and various other ontological questions. It also presents methods to aid understanding of these concepts and to thereby attain spiritual realization.

According to the Zohar, a foundational text for kabalistic thought, Torah study can proceed along four levels of interpretation (exegesis). These four levels are called Pardes because their initial letters spell "PaRDeS" ("Orchard"):

- *Peshat* (lit. "simple"): the direct interpretations of meaning.

- *Remez* (lit. "hint[s]"): the allegoric meanings (through allusion).

- *Derash* (from Heb. *darash* : "inquire" or "seek"): midrashic (Rabbinic) meanings, often with imaginative comparisons with similar words or verses.

- *Sod* (lit. "secret" or "mystery"): the inner, esoteric (metaphysical) meanings, expressed in Kabbalah.

In Kabbalah all Creation unfolds from Divine reality. Kabbalah elaborates a metaphysical structure of emanations from God. In the Kabalistic scheme, God is neither matter nor spirit, but is the creator of both. The question of the Divine nature prompted Kabbalists to envision two aspects of God: (a) God Himself, who is ultimately unknowable, and (b) the revealed aspect of God that created the universe, preserves the universe, and interacts with mankind. Kabbalists speak of the first aspect of God as *Ein Sof*; this is translated as "the infinite", "endless", or "that which has no limits". In this view, nothing can be said about the essence of God. This aspect of God is impersonal. The second aspect of Divine emanations, however, is at least partially accessible to human thought.

The structure of these emanations have been characterized in various ways: Sefirot (Divine attributes) and Partzufim (Divine "faces"); Four Worlds of Creation in a Seder hishtalshelus (Descending Chain of realms), Azilut, Beriyah, Yitzirah, and Asiyah; the Biblical vision by Ezekiel of the Merkabah (Divine angelic "Chariot"). These alternatives are harmonized in subsequent Kabalistic systemization. The central metaphor of Ohr ("Light") is used to describe Divine emanations.

Kabbalists believed that all things are linked to God through these emanations, making all levels in Creation part of one great, gradually descending chain of being. Through this any lower creation reflects its particular characteristics in Supernal Divinity.

The **Sephirot** (singular Sephirah) are the ten emanations and attributes of God with which God continually sustains the universe in existence. The central metaphor of Man's soul is used to describe the Sephirot. This incorporates masculine and feminine aspects, after Genesis 1:27 ("God created man in His own image, in the image of God He created him, male and female He created them"). Corresponding to the last Sephirah in Creation is the indwelling Shechina (Feminine Divine Presence).

According to Lurianic cosmology, the Sephirot correspond to various levels of creation (ten sephirot in each of the Four Worlds , and four worlds within each of the larger four worlds, each containing ten sephirot, which themselves contain ten sephirot, to an infinite number of possibilities,) and are emanated from the Creator for the purpose of creating the universe. The Sephirot are considered revelations of the Creator's will (ratzon), and they should not be understood as ten different "gods" but as ten different ways the one God reveals his will through the Emanations. It is not God who changes but the ability to perceive God that changes.

Altogether 11 sephirot are named. However Keter and Daat are unconscious and conscious dimensions of one principle, conserving 10 forces. The names of the Sephirot in descending order are:

- Keter (supernal crown, representing above-conscious will)
- Chochmah (The highest potential of thought)
- Binah (the understanding of the potential)
- Daat (intellect of knowledge)
- Chesed (sometimes referred to as *Gedolah* -greatness) (loving-kindness)
- Gevurah (sometimes referred to as *Din* -justice or *Pachad* -fear) (severity/strength)
- Rachamim also known as Tiphereth (Mercy)
- Netzach (victory/eternity)
- Hod (glory/splendor)
- Yesod (foundation)
- Malkuth (kingdom)

Divine creation by means of the Ten Sefirot is an ethical process. They represent the different aspects of Morality. Loving-Kindness is a possible moral justification found in Chesed, and Gevurah is the Moral Justification of Justice and both are mediated by Mercy which is Rachamim. However, these pillars of morality become immoral once they become extremes. When Loving-Kindness becomes extreme it can lead to sexual depravity and lack of Justice to the wicked. When Justice becomes extreme, it can lead to torture and the Murder of innocents and unfair punishment.

"Righteous" humans (Tzadikim) ascend these ethical qualities of the Ten Sefirot by doing righteous actions. If there were no "Righteous" humans, the blessings of God would become completely hidden, and creation would cease to exist. While real human actions are the "Foundation" (Yesod) of this universe (Malchut), these actions must accompany the conscious intention of compassion. Compassionate actions are often impossible without "Faith" (Emunah), meaning to trust that God always supports compassionate actions even when God seems hidden. Ultimately, it is necessary to show compassion toward oneself too in order to share compassion toward others. This "selfish" enjoyment of God's blessings but only if in order to empower oneself to assist others, is an important aspect of "Restriction", and is considered a kind of golden mean in Kabbalah, corresponding to the Sefirah of "Adornment" (Tiferet) being part of the "Middle Column".

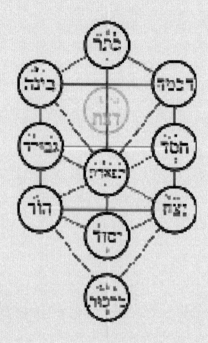

Tree of Life

Tantra

The word Tantra also applies to any of the Hindu scriptures (called "Tantras") commonly identified with the worship of Shakti. Tantra deals primarily with spiritual practices and ritual forms of worship, which aim at liberation from ignorance and rebirth.

David Gordon White offers the following definition: "Tantra is that Asian body of beliefs and practices which, working from the principle that the universe we experience is nothing other than the concrete manifestation of the divine energy of the Godhead that creates and maintains that universe, seeks to ritually appropriate and channel that energy, within the human microcosm, in creative and emancipatory ways."

The Tantric practitioner seeks to use the *prana* (divine power) that flows through the universe (including one's own body) to attain purposeful goals. These goals may be spiritual, material or both. Most practitioners of Tantra consider mystical experience imperative.

In the process of working with energy, the *Tantrika*, or tantric practitioner, has various tools at hand. These include *yoga*, to actuate processes that will "yoke" the practitioner to the divine. Tantrism is a quest for spiritual perfection.

As Robert Svoboda attempts to summarize the three major paths of the Vedic knowledge, he exclaims: " *Because every embodied individual is composed of a body, a mind and a spirit, the ancient Rishis of India who developed the Science of Life organized their wisdom into three bodies of knowledge: Ayurveda, which deals mainly with the physical body; Yoga, which deals mainly with spirit; and Tantra, which is mainly concerned with the mind. The philosophy of all three is identical; their manifestations differ because of their differing emphases. Ayurveda is most concerned with the physical basis of life, concentrating on its harmony of mind and spirit. Yoga controls body and mind to enable them to harmonize with spirit, and Tantra seeks to use the mind to balance the demands of body and spirit.*"

According to Tibetan Buddhist Tantric master Lama Thubten Yeshe:

...each one of us is a union of all universal energy. Everything that we need in order to be complete is within us right at this very moment. It is simply a matter of being able to recognize it. This is the tantric approach.

Thus, the Jindao System converges all the obviously common elements of these philosophical thoughts into one synergistic whole, which aligns our Natural Energetic Healing with Universal Divine Love.

Jindao - The Way of Internal Energy & Strength ™

Experience New Levels of Health, Energy, & Relaxation

A series of Life Transforming Qigong Programs for Energy Healing

"Self Change the Jindao Way" ™

Jindao (勁道) is a complete wellness program (where the Mind, Body, and Spirit are seen as one complete whole), developed from decades of experience, research, and practice. Through this system of synergistic 'energy transformation' programs, you can experience new levels of health, energy, and relaxation.

Jindao Life Transforming Qigong goes beyond healing; it uses holistic and natural energy based transformational therapies that are focused on allowing the "life force" to bring about balance and wellness.

Jindao gives you the necessary tools to help you develop into the fully actualized person that you were meant to be, in a safe and natural way. The system gives you personal insight, transformational energy, and physical strength to prevent you from undermining your own goal pursuit.

Not only will you feel emotionally empowered to succeed, but you will physically feel radiant energy and deep inner strength. Jindao is composed of various complimentary Holistic methods for Self Change, such as:

- Energy Transforming Techniques (Nei Gong);

- Breathing Methods (Qi Gong);

- Chinese Yoga (Dao Yin);

- Inner Strength Building Exercises (Wei Gong);

- Meditation;

- Physical Fitness (Wu Gong);

- Enhanced Energy Diet;

- Taoist, Chan Buddhist, Christian Mysticism, Kabbalist, and Tantric Philosophy;

- Behavioral Science (Recursive Teaching);

- Self Defense (Wu Shu); and more.

Jindao's synergistic approach combines these modalities at once to work the meridian "water pipes" and vessel "reservoirs" both from the inside out and from the outside in, purifying you on all levels. Further, Jindao is the ONLY system that can be used for both health enhancement and for self defense. Whether you're a soccer mom, yoga teacher, reiki healer, massage therapist, or a small business owner and exposed to the stresses of modern day survival. . . Jindao's Qigong and Neigong and other programs enhance anything you're already doing and give life to it.

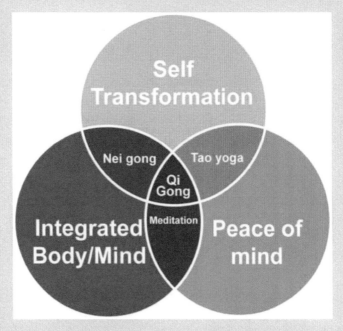

About the Jindao System ™

The Jindao System produces Self Transformation, an Integrated Body / Mind, and Peace of Mind through the use natural movements for enhancing the body's internal energy and strength.

- For the Mind, the Jindao's meditation methods promote calmness and a positive outlook, greatly relieving stress. Attention is given to the role of Eastern Philosophical concepts.

- For the Body, Jindao's Energy Transforming and Inner Strength Building Exercises develop radiant energy, promote inner transformation, and generate a stronger and more limber body. Special attention is given to an energy enhancing diet plan as well.

- For the Spirit, Jindao's Breathing and Meditational Exercises achieve balance by developing Mind-Body-Spirit Awareness so that these elements can be understood as being of one unity, bringing greater focus and clarity.

"Classes are never boring. As a student of martial arts, whether it be for health, longevity or self-defense motivations, Sal fosters ones own awareness of their body, mind and spirit and helps students apply the instruction to their own situation. Over time, one can see their own progress as they achieve deeper levels of their own ability. Progress is cumulative." -- Glenn Keller, Randolph NJ

"Natural Energetic Transformation" ™

Natural Energetic Transformation balances the subtle flow of energy in and around a person. Using the Jindao methods, the nervous system; the muscular-skeletal structure; and the immune system are all worked together at one time to help reverse the aging process, boost health and vitality, and promote longevity and total wellness.

Gentle, natural exercises are performed to increase and balance the flow of energy through the body. The internal movements also develop balance, coordination, flexibility, muscle strength, and endurance.

Deep breathing is coordinated with the movements to promote relaxation and develop the mind-body connection.

This leads to the enhancement of physical, mental, and spiritual health. "Natural Energetic Transformation" occurs that provide relief from chronic aches and pains, negative feelings, and malfunctioning immune systems.

Great exercises for **Senior Fitness**! Reverses the aging process - the secret to feeling better and living longer. Regular exercise can prevent or delay diabetes and heart trouble. It can also reduce arthritis pain, anxiety, and depression. It can help older people stay independent.

Energy Transforming and Breathing Exercises

The program's Natural Energetic Transforming exercises are based on ancient Qigong (Chi Gung) and Neigong movements that help balance the body from the inside out, producing three major changes in the body:

1. Helps to rid the body of stagnant energy that is not moving freely. Stagnant energy is located where there are physical, emotional, mental, and psychic blockages.

2. Raises the body's energy levels so that its own natural healing capacities are stimulated and become strongly elevated.

3. Helps to balance the body's energy flow through the meridians and deeper energy channels and vessels.

The famous Dr. Oz, Oprah's medical guru, on his television program, also espoused qigong as a way to "add years to your life", reduce stress, promote longevity, cardiovascular care, and help alleviate chronic pain and fatigue symptoms.

Qigong makes your body pulse with energy. Only Qigong deals with the actual energy itself to such a degree that it causes our body to regenerate.

People who work with Reiki Healing, Healing Touch, Massage, Yoga, and other related modalities can greatly benefit from our programs by enhancing their energy sensibilities.

Success Stories

"I was also told that it would be difficult to have kids with the built up scar tissue from surgery many years earlier. . . The qigong taught along with the Kung Fu forms helped tone my body and got me back on the road to a better shape and manage my stress. I felt different on many levels after each class. A year later I was able to have a child, in fact now I have two. Without Sal, I could not start to make positive changes for my life and benefit from them now." -- Laura Keiles, NJ

Inner Strength Building Exercises

The program's Inner Strength Building Exercises, known as Weigong, are based on ancient Natural Internal Arts that help strengthen the body from the outside in.

There are four main types of exercise and all people, especially seniors, need some of each:

1. Endurance & Stamina activities, which build "staying power" and improve the health of the heart and circulatory system.

2. Strengthening exercises which build muscle tissue and reduce age-related muscle loss.

3. Stretching exercises to keep the body limber and flexible.

4. Balance exercises to reduce the chances of a fall.

These techniques and postural movements are done efficiently and effectively using core body mechanics and correct alignment. Efficiently and effectively means it will be done intelligently and quickly without wasted energy or efforts by using brute force.

The postural movements develop and maintain strength, flexibility, sharp reflexes, self-confidence, and self-control. Also, Motor skills are greatly enhanced.

Correct posture, body alignment, and core body mechanics are emphasized.

Success Stories

"I started the class in poor physical condition with a lot of tendon and cartilage damage in my ankles and knees. The combination of the Qi gong class, Kung Fu class and the additional exercises that Sal had taught me had made a marked improvement in my lifestyle. I have typically been on crutches or had to use ankle braces about every 6 months for over ten years due to recurring injuries, but since I have been practicing the material that Sal taught I have been brace free for about three years now. I think this is in part due to increased strength of my body from the Qi gong exercises, but mostly to the fact that the Kung Fu movements have thought me how to properly move my body without causing injury." -- Brett D'Alessio, Califon NJ

"When I first came to the class keeping my knee over the toe was difficult because I had weak muscles. The classes taught by Sal helped me gain muscle tone without going to a gym " -- Bruce Christman, Parsippany NJ

Our Qigong & Neigong Programs are ideal for stress reduction, chronic pain, and aging issues. Great for staying calm, centered, grounded, and relaxed in the workplace or at home. Increases productivity and focus. (Corporate classes available)

Do you have any of the following symptoms?

- Joint pain
- Inflammation
- Stiffness
- Back pain
- Arthritis
- Osteoporosis
- Weakness in muscles
- Gastric / intestinal problems
- Cardio Vascular problems
- Aging problems
- headaches from tension
- Over weight
- Fatigue
- Low energy
- Lack of sleep
- Rundown
- Negative feelings
- Apathy, boredom
- Loss of focus or purpose
- Lack of confidence
- Lack of control
- Anger
- Anxiety
- Stressful environment or lifestyle.

If you answered yes to any of those questions, then you can benefit from the Jindao system, which:

- Promotes physical & emotional healing
- Reverses the aging process
- Boosts health and vitality
- Promotes longevity & total wellness
- Prevents further Osteoporosis
- Develops fitness
- Aids in weight loss
- Heals internal injuries
- Reduces inflammation
- Alleviate joint pain
- Exercises the internal organs
- Improves digestion and elimination
- Enhances detoxification
- Strengthens blood circulation
- Gains confidence and self control
- Better able to focus
- Energizes body, mind, and spirit
- Gain peace of mind
- Relieves stress & tension
- Increases stamina
- Builds strength
- Improves daily performance
- Improves motor skills
- Increase mind-body awareness
- Increases coordination
- Protect self and loved ones
- Improves sports skills & abilities
- and more!
- Our Inner Energy and Strength programs (Qigong, Neigong, Daoyin, and more) are for **EVERY ONE,** young, old, well, and ill.

- People in good health can augment and strengthen their wellbeing, and ill or sick people can boost their body's vital force and transform themselves.

- They are also very beneficial for Holistic healing physicians, such as acupuncturists; chiropractors; physical therapists; mental health doctors such as psychotherapists and psychologists; as well as for all types of Energy Healers, such as massage therapists, Reiki masters; Teachers, Writers, Tai Chi, Yoga, Meditation, Martial arts practitioners, etc.

Although Qi Gong was introduced to the Western world a few decades ago, it has been practiced for thousands of years in China and has been gaining popularity in the United States and Europe recently. Many hospitals and rehabilitation institutions have incorporated this transformational art form into their therapy programs.

For those who sit or stand in one position for lengthy amounts of time, it is important to learn and practice qi gong to give your body a "break". When Qi is stuck inside your body, you will feel "stuck" both physically and emotionally. The key to keeping a healthy body is to let the Qi flow through your body, bringing and maintaining vitality.

Dr. Oz endorses Qigong!

"If you want to be healthy and live to 100, do Qigong ."
- Dr. Mehmet Oz

Dr. Oz , Oprah's favorite MD, was asked out of all the health practices that one could do, what was the one practice that he would choose and recommend people practice to stay healthy. His response: If you want to be healthy and live to 100, do Qigong. He added that Qigong reverses the aging process.

On another Oprah show, Dr. Oz interviewed a couple who had been very overweight with many illnesses. Previously, he started them onto a program of better nutrition and a Qigong practice. They lost much of their excess weight, improved their energy, decreased most medication, and slowed their aging process. These improvements are attributed to Qigong and eating better.

Do you desire a change in your life?

Do you want a better quality of life?

Do you want to turn back the clock?

Are you facing a health challenge?

Do you want more wealth & happiness?

Jindao Life Transforming Qigong is a holistic system of special energy healing programs for powerful self transformation.

Our programs allow you to:

- Eliminate long held unresolved anger and grief.

- Develop superior fitness and vitality.

- Achieve peace of mind, focus, and clear insight.

- Reverse the aging process.

- Develop into the fully actualized person that you were meant to be.

- Feel happier, energized, and powerful.

- Become more efficient and effective.

The **Jindao Life Transforming Qigong System** is a family of wellness practices for health, fitness, energy development, and stress relief. These practices include moving exercises, as well as a number of other practices such as standing and sitting meditations, massage, therapeutic healing techniques, and other health and energy-building practices. The Jindao System converges different material into one holistic energy healing therapy.

Great for natural healing of Osteoporosis, Osteopenia, Arthritis, Asthma, Shoulder and Back pain, and more.

We offer a series of special Qigong, Neigong, and Weigong programs. Advanced concepts are explained in everyday language, augmented with practice exercises, and demonstrated through practical applications that can apply to both Qigong health enhancement but also to self defense. This is the ONLY Qigong program available that teaches also the hidden protection aspects of Qigong movements and postures.

Most importantly, instruction will be given in HOW to feel the movements by using the deeper muscles, correct body mechanics, correct body alignment, and correct rooting. Information is also given on WHY movements are done so. Over 30 years of research and experience has been done to develop the course materials for this program!

Program 1. Self Healing & Purifying Qigong Basics - Experience new levels of health, energy, and relaxation with self healing exercises to integrate your body and mind.

This is a 3 month program where you will learn foundational Taoist and Buddhist self healing methods.

Program 2. Self Transforming Shaolin Neigong - Develop superior inner energy and strength.

This is a 6 month program where you will learn internal techniques for physical, emotional, and spiritual wellbeing and self defense. Program 1 must be completed as a prerequisite.

Program 3 - Peace of Mind Taoist Neigong - Recharge your life to be free of physical, emotional, and spiritual burdens.

This is a 6 month program where you will learn internal techniques for physical, emotional, and spiritual wellbeing and peace of mind. Program 1 or 2 must be completed as a prerequisite.

Program 4 - Natural Chinese Internal Martial Arts & Self Defense - Learn the most efficient and effective Shaolin and Taoist Natural internal martial arts and Weigong conditioning.

This is an ongoing program where you will learn internal and external exercises for mastering Natural Chinese Martial Arts and Self Defense. Program 1 and 2 is recommended as a prerequisite.

Program 5 - Advanced Healing Qigong - Various Qigong exercises that allow you to quickly activate and strongly radiate your healing energy. You can move Qi throughout the body to perform full body cleansing that removes emotional as well as physical blockages. Includes free-form walking Qigong merging different methods.

Special 1 day Workshops and 2-3 day Seminars - an ongoing series of events featuring specialized topics in the internal arts. Cost depends on material and length of event.

Also, private Qigong Training classes and Qigong healing sessions are available.

For appointments and information, contact the instructor: Sal Canzonieri, please call 973-599-9640 or contact via email: salcanzonieri@att.net

---

**Energy Healing Sessions** –   **(up to 90 minutes) – weekly, 3-6 sessions**

Healing movements done for unblocking your body's energy gates and to promote wellness. **Illness, injury, or stress can cause blockages in one or more gates through which energy flows.** When that happens, energy backs up and stagnates above the blocked point and the energy flow is restricted to points below the blockages. Blockages almost always result in **PAIN or ILLNESS.**

**Tui Na – Chinese Massage Sessions** –   **(30-60 minutes)**

Deep massaging and body drumming movements done for unblocking your body's energy gates and to promote wellness . Tui Na ("Push & Grab") kneads the muscles, opens the joints to increase synovial fluid, and relieves tension.

See the following for detailed Program descriptions:

Program 1 - Self Healing Qigong Fundamentals

Experience new levels of health, energy, and relaxation.

This is a 3 month program in which the foundational material for learning self healing will be taught.

Your results for participating in this program will be:

- Proper breathing methods will be mastered.

- Proper body posture and alignment will be mastered.

- Basic self healing methods will be mastered.

- You will be able to integrate your body and mind.

- You will feel healthier, stronger, and more energetic.

The curriculum for Program 1 includes the following Taoist & Buddhist Self Healing Qigong material:

Introduction - foundational material

Foundational sitting, standing, stretching, conditioning, and strengthening movements that prepare one for the later lessons.

Opening the Mind-Body Awareness

The focus is on opening both your body and mind. On the physical side, works on flexibility, range of motion, and easy movements to open and lengthen all parts of your body. Movements also stimulate all the major energy systems in your body. To open your mind, we'll teach you an effective stress-relief and relaxation technique, plus a simple Qi energy awareness practice.

A. Active Qigong - To open the body, we use primarily movements in the limbs to open up the spine, hips and legs, and arms and shoulders.

1. Ba Duan Jin 八段錦 **(8 Section Brocade):**

As an introduction to Taoist Qigong, some simple and easy to learn standing and moving movements are taught in a series of eight postures. Aids in aligning, stretching, conditioning, balancing, and strengthening the body. This exercise is very ancient and is both Taoist and Buddhist influenced.

1. Hold the Sky with Both Palms
2. Draw Bow to Shoot a Hawk
3. Touch Heaven and Earth
4. Looking Backward
5. Wag Head and Tail
6. Opening the Spine
7. Punch with Tiger Eyes
8. Raise Heels.

2. Whole Body Breathing Qigong

3. Healing Qigongs:

- Lower the Qi & Cleanse the Organs
- Embrace Moon standing meditation
- Snake standing meditation

- One Finger "Zen" / Chan Qigong (with sound)

- Recharging Qigong (great for health practitioners!)

4. Purifying Qi:

- Bone Marrow Cleansing Qigong

- Six Healing Sounds Neigong

5. Gathering & Circulating Qi

- Standing Meditation
- Walking Meditation - Mo Cha Bu (Rubbing Steps)
- Opening & Closing Steps

6. Dispersing Stagnation Massage (dantian, kidneys, etc.)

B. Passive Qigong - seated or standing activates hands and feet points.

Various Qigong methods are taught, some simple and easy to learn standing and moving movements. Aids in connecting the mind with the body. These exercises are very ancient and are both Taoist and Buddhist influenced.

1. Falling Water Qigong – To open the mind, focuses on draining stagnant Qi from the hands and feet.

C. Qi Emission - focuses on generating and feeling Qi in the palms.

1. Following Qigong – sensitivity & awareness training. Single arm and double arm methods.

2. Interactive Qigong – generate greater Qi feeling & awareness:

A. Qi Generating Neigong

1. Stand in Wuji
2. Holding Balloon
3. Horizontal Dantian Rotation
4. Vertical Dantian Rotation
5. Horizontal Qi Pull
6. Vertical Qi Pull
7. Exchanging Qi
8. Return to Wuji.

B. Three Circle Yin & Yang Meridians Neigong

C. Triple Warmer Neigong

D. Alleviation of Triple Warmers

E. Balance Stomach & Spleen (White Crane Spreads Wings)

Coordinate Body, Mind & Breath

The focus is on physical coordination that will teach you how to use your body in an integrated fashion and on coordinating movement, breathing, and mental concentration to increase the benefits you get from Qigong. Combining these three elements creates a synergistic effect, allowing greater levels of health enhancement and fitness, while also boosting the immune system.

Active & Passive Qigong

1. Constant Bear Qigong – This exercise works the waist, hips, and legs using a combination of turning and weight shifting.

2. Reverse Bear Qigong – This exercise adds in 'silk reeling' (staying connected as weight transfers from one side to other).

3. Embrace the Pearl Qigong – Standing exercise done without movement in order to focus concentration with breathing. Accumulates and restores energy in body.

4. Lifting Water Qigong - tool for learning relaxed arm movement using deeper muscles without tension.

5. Spiraling Qigong - increases mobility, flexibility, and coordination of arms and torso, while relieving muscular tension.

Rooting and Energetics

Rooting is the single most basic concept in all of neigong and internal martial arts. Rooting involves keeping both a physical and an energetic connection to the ground for stability, balance, and centering. Also, focus on 'Tai Ji Energetics', giving you the experiences of working with Qi both inside and outside of the body.

1. Isolated Spine Stretch - develops awareness of the upper body structures, primarily the spine.

2. Water pump Qigong - develops awareness of the lower body structures, the hips and legs.

3. Three Circle Qigong – standing neigong for rooting and and actively circulating Qi throughout the body.

4. Universal Post Qigong – neigong for physically and energetically developing rooting in legs and feet, while being single weighted in Cat Stance.

5. Circling Hands Qigong – various advanced exercises for rooting the lower body while in Bow Stance and spiraling the upper body circulating Qi (Cloud Hands, Wave Hands Like Clouds, Flower Hidden in Mirror, etc.).

Four Energies Neigong and Centering Elements Qigong - integrates the whole mind-body with flowing standing and walking movements. Centering Qigong connects to the energy fields of the Five Elements and energizes and harmonizes these areas for physical, mental, and spiritual health.

Wai Dan Methods, by focusing on the meridian "water pipes" help keep energy flowing smoothly through the body for health, stress relief, and well-being. They use the *limbs* to encourage smooth qi flow through the *meridians*. As qi builds up in the limbs during practice, it will eventually flow back through the meridians to the internal organs to nourish them. Any excess of qi in the meridians will be "siphoned"; off into the vessel "reservoirs"; for storage. Level 1 primarily uses Waidan methods.

Nai Dan Methods, by focusing on the vessel "reservoirs" help develop abundant energy for the entire body. They use primarily *torso* movements, especially in the major joints such as the shoulders or hip sockets, and/or mental concentration to generate and store qi in the *reservoirs*. As abundant qi becomes available, it will "overflow"; the reservoirs into the meridians, helping to clear out obstructions and smooth out qi flow. Levels 2 -4 primarily use Naidan and Waidan / Naidan hybrid methods.

Program 2 - Self Transforming Shaolin Neigong

Develop superior inner energy and strength.

(Note: To enter Program 2, you must have either completed Program 1 - Self Healing Qigong Basics OR must be able to demonstrate mastery of basics based on prior experience)

This is a 6 month program in which internal exercises for superior physical, emotional, and spiritual wellbeing and self defense will be taught.

The curriculum for Program 2 includes the following Shaolin Life Transforming Neigong material:

Preparation Exercises:

1. Shaolin Preparation Qigong -

• Rub hands – stimulate 'Laogong' (human gate) energy points in palm centers.
• Energize temples – press warm palms to temples.
• Washing the face - warm hands and rub palms from top to bottom and back (24x)
• Tap the head – tap fingers gently over skull and temple areas.
• Tap the central body – tap fists from breastbone to abdomen.
• Tap legs and arms – taps fists over lower back and over front and back of legs and arms.
• Develop Qi attentiveness – slowly raise & lower each arm with attention to Laogong points.
• Stand on Tightrope – develop balance & concentration, arms out, arms in, and arms crossed.

2. Shaolin Qigong - set of breathing exercises with moving arms

- Tu Na or Tugu Naxin qigong
- Opening qigong
- Marriage of Heaven & Earth qigong
- Letting Go qigong
- Closing qigong.

3. Important Internal Exercises -

• Opening/closing the kua – Taiji Swings 1-3
• Rooting exercises (follow ground path)
• Peng Jin exercises (rubber ball power)
• Whole Body exercises – 'Bend Bow Shoot Arrow' exercise
• Spiral movement exercises (silk reeling energy)

To build a strong foundation, three Shaolin Qigong moving methods are taught that are part of the Shaolin Rou Gong system:

Shaolin Rou Gong 少林 柔功 **(Soft or Supple Exercises) System -** Shaolin Rou Qong is also known as Shaolin Taiji Quan.

1. Shaolin Liu He Gong 少林 六合功 (6 Harmony Exercises)

Composed of 6 sets of special walking qigong movements that unite breathing methods, acupuncture points and meridians, body mechanics, and self defense movements. The 6 Harmony movements are considered the primary foundation to all long fist applications, and the main starting point for the internal version of Shaolin martial arts. Each of the 6 exercises covers different vessels and meridians of the body (such as the Lungs, Spleen, Liver, Triple Burners, Heart, and Kidneys). The main function of the 6 Harmony is to:
- relieve anxiety, stress, and depression;
- aid in mental health;
- balance the emotions;
- cleanse stagnation in the body;
- increase respiratory capacity;
- strengthen the joints and ligaments of the body;
- and begin to correctly use Shaolin body mechanics that bridge to Tai Ji Quan (swing, sink, and point).

1. Single Hand Pushes Mountain -- Dan Shou Tui Shan (lungs)

2. Wind Swings Willow -- Feng Bai Yang-Liu (spleen)

3. Chest center hugs Moon -- Huai Zhong Bao Yue (liver)

4. Hide Tiger posture (single palm presses down) -- Fu Hu Shi (triple burner)

5. Lift Palm to Sky -- Tuo Tien Zhang (heart)

6. Subdue Dragon & Tiger Palm -- Jiang Long Zhang (kidneys).

2. Shaolin Chan Yuan Gong 少林 禪圓功 (Zen Circular Exercises)

Composed of a series of 8-10 demanding internal movements and postures. These movements are made to:
- teach one to connect the upper and lower body into one functioning unit;
- stimulate and balance the body's meridian channels;
- strengthen the waist / hip (kua in Chinese) inguinal fold area;
- improve posture and back/spine structural problems;
- increase internal strength and stamina;
- generate energy;
- and bridge between Shaolin and Tai Ji Quan (such as Brush Knee Twist Step and other movements);
- self defense version of the exercise set exists as well.

1. Avoid (evade) Sun, Hide (conceal) Clouds -- Bi Ri Zhe Yun (6x)
2. (Greet) In the Wind, Wipe Dirt -- Ying-Feng Hui Chen (6x)
3. Forcibly Split Hua Mountain -- Li Pi Hua Shan (6x)
4. Move against Water-row (current) Boat -- Ni Shui Xing Zhou (8x)

5. Autumn Wind Sweeps Leaves (Twist Waist move around Hips) -- Qiu Feng Sao Ye (Niu Yao Zhou Kua) (8x)
6. Shake Body Sway Shoulders -- Yao Shen Huang Bang (8x)
7. Forcibly Pull Nine Bulls -- Li La Jiu Niu (8x).

3. Shaolin Luohan 13 Gong 少林 罗汉十三功 (Arhat 13 Exercises)

Composed of a series of 13 complex movements and postures. The movements:
- emphasize the correct way to use the internal concepts of Yielding, Sinking, Absorbing, Transferring, and Pointing energy for both health and self defense.
- combine the powers of meditation and movement into one smooth practice
- are vigorous and feature special stepping patterns that are a bridge to Tai Ji Quan and Xing Yi stepping methods.
- are made to enhance emotional health, vitality, muscle tone, internal strength, and internal cleansing of the bowels.
- are a link to ancient Taoist methods also known as the Tai Ji 13 Gung, and Buddhist yogic movements originally from India.
- also a powerful self defense set containing all these movements and some additional transitional movements that feature the full 18 Luohans.

1. Old Monk Chops Wood

2. Lazy Drapes on Coat

3. Sleepy Monk Lies on Pillow

4. Double Hands Push Mountain

5. Wind Shakes the Lotus Leaves

6. Luohan Bears the Flag

7. Seven Star Striking Fist

8. Hug Tiger's Head

9. Roll Hands, Push Palm

10. Luohan Sifts Flour

11. Snake Flashes Tongue

12. Insert Incense

13. Old Monk Carries Basket on Arm.

After learning and MASTERING all 3 Rou Gong sets, the student will be able to have the CORRECT body mechanics and internal energy development and movement necessary to truly understand and perform the most ancient and traditional methods of the Shaolin system and support a strong foundation for mastering the other internal arts of Tai Ji Quan, Xing Yi, and Ba Gua Zhang.

Program 3 - Peace of Mind Taoist Neigong

Recharge your life to be free of physical, emotional, and spiritual burdens.

(Note: To enter Program 3, you must have either completed Program 1 Self Healing Qigong Basics OR must be able to demonstrate mastery of basics based on prior experience)

1. Standing Mediation - various standing post neigong.

2. Walking Meditation - straight-line walking versions of standing post neigong

3. Circle Walking Meditation - circle walking meditation neigong and stepping methods.

Program 4 - Natural Chinese Internal Martial Arts & Self Defense

Learn the most efficient and effective Shaolin and Taoist Natural internal martial arts and Weigong conditioning.

This is an ongoing program.

Qigong & Neigong Workshops & Seminars

1 day Workshops and 2-3 day Seminars - an ongoing series of events featuring specialized topics in the internal arts. This is a 12 month program in which specialized internal exercises for physical, emotional, and spiritual wellbeing will be taught.

CONTACT INFORMATION:

Sal Canzonieri - Jindao Life Transforming Qigong Instruction and Healing

Email: salcanzonieri@att.net

Website: www.JinDaoLife.com

Author & Instructor Information:

Mr. Salvatore (Sal) Canzonieri has a BA degree in Behavioral Science (triple major in Psychology, Sociology, and Anthropology, with a Concentration (Thesis) on 'Subcultures and Societal Change' from Drew University in Madison, NJ.

Mr. Canzonieri has been practicing traditional Chinese martial arts and since 1975 in such styles as Shuai Jiao (Chinese art of takedowns), Tong Bei, Shaolin, Taizu Chang Quan, Yue Jia Quan (Ba Fan Shou), Xing Yi, Tai Ji Quan, Ba Gua Zhang, and others. He began learning and practicing Qigong / Neigong since 1980.

He has been a certified instructor since 1998 by the **International Congress of Oriental Medicine and Martial Arts** to represent the state of New Jersey in Chinese Qigong and Internal Martial Arts.

From the mid 1980s, he studied Kabbalism, both Jewish and Christian, for many years at various schools in the New York / New Jersey area. He also studied Christian Mysticism and related philosophies for many years as well.

During the 1980s and 90s, he also studied nutritional healing with Gary Null, Dr. Atkins, and various others.

He has been conducting research in the history of traditional Chinese martial arts styles for over 20 years and is most known for his history based articles in various martial arts magazines, such as "Kung Fu Qi Gung" magazine, "Han Wei" magazine, and other publications all over the world (translated in Spanish, Italian, Russian, and Chinese languages).

Mr. Canzonieri has also judged routines for 5 years during the 1990s at the Han Wei Martial Arts Tournaments.

He also taught for over 20 years Qigong / Neigong and Martial Art classes for the Diversity Program and the Employee Health Program, at Bell Laboratories - Lucent Technologies, on ancient Shaolin methods of Qi Gung, Self Defense, and empty hand sets.

In the year 2000, Mr. Canzonieri won a Theodore Vail Award (for saving person's life using his Neigong knowledge).

Currently, Mr. Canzonieri is the chief instructor of The Whippany Kung Fu Club and the Natural Chinese Martial Arts & Qigong School of NJ (over 20 years), and resides in New Jersey, USA.

Mr. Canzonieri, is now accepting new students for a weekly daytime evening program, named "Jindao - The Way of Internal Energy and Strength" TM, featuring Natural Traditional Chinese Qigong and Martial Arts, which includes Qi Gung energy exercises ("Chinese yoga") for health and relaxation, stretching and conditioning, self defense, sports skills improvement, and more.

He also is available for Qigong and Self Defense seminars in the USA and overseas.

Mr. Canzonieri taught Shaolin Neigong and Self Defense seminars in Valencia Spain in 2008 and 2009; and many private classes and seminars in Canada, New York City, New Jersey, Chicago IL, California, and Texas in the USA.

Seminars and Private lessons are available, please contact via email: salcanzonieri@att.net or call: 973-599-9640

Among Salvatore's classroom, seminar, and private Qigong and Martial Art instructor's (between 1975 and 2008) have been Al Simon (Qigong, TJQ), Bruce Franztis (Qigong, Neigong, TJQ, BGZ), Lin Chihyung (Qigong, Shaolin, Tongbei, Shuaijiao, Chang Quan, Chuaojiao, Fanzi Quan, Tanglang, Sunbin, TJQ, XY, BGZ), Frank Allen (TJQ, BGZ, XY), Charles Chen Chang-Lin (Wu Tan School), Paul Muller (Qigong, CLF, Shaolin, Karate), Peter Kwok's students (Chang Quan, Hua Quan, etc.), Warner Ollie (BP Chan's Chen TJQ), Tang Jin Ping (various Northern Chinese martial arts), Yang Jing Ming, Albert Chu (Qigong), Ming Sheuh (Shaolin Quan), various members of the Whippany Bell Labs Kung Fu club (Luohan Shaolin, Song Taizu Quan, and other Northern and Southern Chinese martial arts), and various others. Also, over 20 years correspondence with Qigong and Chinese martial artist researchers and practitioners from Mainland China, Taiwan, Europe, South America, Russia, and elsewhere.